THE KINGDOM OF GOD

Five Lectures

J. W. Rogerson

BEAUCHIEF
ABBEY·PRESS

Published by Beauchief Abbey Press.
Copyright © J W Rogerson, 2015
ISBN 978-0-9576841-6-4

CONTENTS

INTRODUCTION

This book is about a puzzle and a challenge.

It is also about our central experiences as human beings.

Jesus of Nazareth proclaims the arrival of something called 'The Kingdom of Heaven' and this calls into question everyday assumptions about power, purpose, relationships, individuality and community. The puzzle concerns questions about why the dynamic and centrality of the Kingdom as proclaimed by Jesus has found so little space in the creeds and doctrines of the Church. In the following pages you can explore Jesus's central message in the company of a world-class scholar.

The five chapters of this book were given by John Rogerson as the 2014 Beauchief Abbey lectures. Their publication by Beauchief Abbey Press marks the congregation's desire to provide wider public access to the work of Prof. Rogerson. His voice is unusual in British culture because he is both an Anglican priest and an international academic celebrated for insights into the modern social relevance of the Old Testament and research into the history of European Biblical scholarship.

This body of work highlights ways in which the development of Biblical criticism, with its uneasy (and still bumpy) unpacking in Britain, provides insights and help to a modern faith which seeks to be honest, open, intellectually and philosophically robust and yet still an unwaveringly dynamic traditional Christianity. The major 20th century Christian philosopher Paul Tillich mused in some late reflections

> the story of Biblical criticism is one of the greatest stories of man's intellectual history, equal to the growth of modern science [1]

and John Rogerson's career has made a significant contemporary contribution to the development and public understanding of that intellectual history. The rigour and intellectual reach of the biblical scholar is present throughout this current book and we are familiar at Beauchief Abbey with the idea sometimes expressed in his sermons that nothing ought to be feared by individuals and communities in seeking the truth. The intellect is not something to be left at the church door. The unexpected and transformative offer of faith appeals deeply to both heart and mind. The kingdom of God is an offer for all our human attributes and qualities.

This book introduces a culture that engages both our emotions and our capacity to reason – it speaks to our intelligence and our experiences. The first chapter includes references to British writers Ruskin, Clutton-Brock, C.S. Lewis, and J. Heywood Thomas who have explored this theme in the context of wider European intellectual traditions. The influential work of Rudolph Otto is also discussed:

> ... in 1917, the German theologian Rudolf Otto had published his book 'The Idea of the Holy', a work that has had a

---

[1] Paul Tillich, Personal Introduction to My Systematic Theology, published posthumously in *Modern Theology*, vol. 1, issue 2, 1985.

profound influence upon the study of religion in general. Otto described and analysed human experiences in which there was an encounter with what Otto variously called 'the holy', 'the wholly other', and the 'numinous'. In each case the result of such an encounter was to make a person aware of being confronted by something that was so much more real than his own being, something that could fill him with awe and wonder.

A significant earlier British explorer of this territory was the poet and writer Samuel Taylor Coleridge (1772 – 1834). Coleridge's seminal influence on the development of English culture in the 19th century is little appreciated today, and this forms the basis of a separate Beauchief Abbey inspired project in 2016. But Coleridge's importance does not escape the notice of Rudolf Otto, and in unpublished notes from 1931 written as an introduction the English language edition of his book *The Philosophy of Religion based on Kant and Fries*, Otto expresses the hope that his writing will find a sympathetic readership in the home land of S. T. Coleridge:

> It appears to me that Coleridge in his poems had already reached such a clear vision of the factor of the "Numinous" and had so clearly expressed this vision, that to readers of this poet my book on *The Idea of the Holy* could scarcely offer much that was novel. [2]

These unpublished notes presumably arrived too late for inclusion in the printed body of the 1931 English language edition of *The Philosophy of Religion* and were inserted by the publisher as a loose-leaf addendum. This single sheet fell from a 1st edition copy of *The Philosophy of Religion* during a recent research project and its neglected contents have caused

---

[2] R. Otto, Unpublished notes for *The Philosophy of Religion based on Kant and Fries*, London, 1931 (English translation of his *Kantische- Fries'sche Religionsphilosophie*, Tübingen, 1909).

surprise and interest. We have taken the opportunity to print the full text of this missing English introduction by Otto as an appendix to this book, which can be found on page 85.

Otto's brief notes are a plea that non-rational and rational factors be taken seriously and together as important and essential elements of religion. He writes only seven brief notes for an English reading audience but, none-the-less, things can be said so compactly and profoundly in a fragment, as Coleridge himself knew. In these short paragraphs Rudolf Otto finds space to bring together De Wette, Schleiermacher, Fries, Coleridge, the Anglican Humanistic Fathers and the tension between specific and general revelation. Even his comments on technical translations of theological and philosophical German words into English speak to the gallery. It is hoped that 84 years after he wrote these notes for English readers Otto will again find a receptive and grateful audience.

In the lectures that follow on from the first chapter, John Rogerson explores how ideas of The Kingdom are held in Old Testament literature, and then proceeds to outline the offer and challenge of the Kingdom of God in the teaching of Jesus, and its subsequent handling and development in the New Testament writings of Paul and John. The last lecture deals with the role of the church today. Here we discover the challenge.

This is a personal book. It deals at an intellectual level with the importance of religious experience and thought, but is also illustrated with insights from John Rogerson's own career. A recurring theme heard in his sermons and ministry at Beauchief Abbey underpins the writing of this book, and in spite of John's formidable international learning and academic reputation, getting to grips with the territory he has served as a scholar reveals, surprisingly to some of us perhaps, that God is not a theory to be argued over and understood, but the living presence of the creator spirit, best appreciated through our desire for right relationships, through news of the Kingdom, and in those experiences and ideas narrated in the life, teaching, betrayal, execution and continuing influence of Jesus.

I take this opportunity to add personal thanks to John for his work and support of the community at Beauchief Abbey. A previous lecture series of his on the Kingdom of Heaven in 2008 made a considerable impression on me and others. This has altered the course of my work and led to the founding of the Beauchief Abbey Press.

What follows is a splendid introduction to the disruptive dynamic and dimension of 'the kingdom of heaven'. It begins with the provocative theme:

Is news of the kingdom of heaven a well-kept secret?

R M PARRY
Penarth, May 2015

PREFACE

The Kingdom of God is a topic that has interested me for many years, and indeed it was the study of this subject that helped me to find my way into Christian faith. I was therefore delighted when I was invited to give the 2014 Beauchief Abbey Lent Lectures on this topic.

The lectures are printed here exactly as they were delivered. They were also videoed and can be viewed via the Beauchief Abbey Congregation web site. Their publication will enable the text to be considered more carefully than is possible with an oral presentation. I hope very much that the lectures will whet the appetite of readers to explore the subject further for themselves because, obviously, such a vast and important subject cannot be adequately covered in five short lectures.

The lectures express something of the ethos of Beauchief Abbey, as is explained in the final lecture, and it is appropriate that the lectures appear under the imprint of Beauchief Abbey Press.

J. W. Rogerson

LECTURE 1

"What is the Kingdom of God?"

The title of this evening's lecture is 'what is the kingdom of God'; however, I shall spend most of my time this evening talking not about the kingdom of God, but about the kingdom of heaven, so I need to begin by explaining why. In the New Testament, as I shall say later, the two terms 'kingdom of God' and 'kingdom of heaven' refer to exactly the same thing. There is no difference in meaning between them. In this lecture, however, I shall be using them in a different way from what occurs in the New Testament. I shall use the two terms to describe the same thing, but the same thing viewed from two quite different angles. By 'kingdom of God' I shall mean something that is described in the Bible, especially in the teaching and preaching of Jesus. By 'kingdom of heaven' I shall mean something that is not necessarily religious, but which is definitely spiritual. I hope that the importance of the distinction will become clear as the lecture proceeds.

I begin, then, with a book entitled 'What is the Kingdom of Heaven?' by the art critic and writer Arthur Clutton-Brock (1868-1924). In it, Clutton-Brock imagines an intelligent inquirer seeking an answer to the question 'what is the kingdom of heaven?'[3] Because he has come across the phrase 'kingdom of heaven' in the teaching of Jesus in the New Testament, the inquirer assumes that if he wants to discover what it is, he will find the answer in the teachings of the church which was founded by Jesus. So he goes to look at the creeds. What does the Apostles' Creed, which is recited at morning and evening prayer, say about the kingdom of heaven? It does not mention it at all! Perhaps the Nicene Creed, which is recited at Holy Communion, says something about it. No, there is no mention here, either. The inquirer now turns to the 39 Articles of Religion. These, after all, are the official statement of the doctrine of the Church of England, and when I was ordained I was required to give to them 'general assent'. So what do they say about the kingdom of heaven? Again, and amazingly, there is no mention in the Articles of that subject which was at the centre of the teaching and preaching of Jesus. Even more astonishingly, article XXXV, which lists 21 Homilies which, according to the article, should be 'read in churches by the ministers, diligently and distinctly, that they may be understanded of the people', does not include any reference to the kingdom of heaven among the titles of the Homilies that are listed. In fact, the only mention of the kingdom of heaven that the inquirer discovers is in the Catechism, where it is stated that at baptism a child becomes a child of God, and an inheritor of the kingdom of heaven. However, there is no explanation as to what this might mean. Not surprisingly, the inquirer is in deep despair. If he had been able to read German he might have been directed to the Greater Catechism of Martin Luther where, in an exposition of the phrase in the Lord's Prayer 'thy kingdom come', Luther

---

[3] A. Clutton-Brock, *What is the Kingdom of Heaven?*, London: Methuen, 1919.

explains that the kingdom is something that has been established by the ministry and death of Jesus, that it has destroyed the kingdom of the devil and that believers are no longer ultimately subject to it.[4] However, Clutton-Brock does not refer his inquirer to Luther, and neither shall we, but shall follow Clutton-Brock's attempts to answer his own question.

His main observation is that the kingdom of heaven is a relationship, but not a relationship of use. This needs to be spelled out. We all possess many objects whose value to us is their usefulness. A car owner may be very proud of the model he possesses. It may embrace the latest technology or, alternatively, be a vintage car of great rarity. However, if it does not go, if it cannot take him to where he wishes to drive or, in the case of a vintage car, cannot take part in vintage car rallies, it has very little value. Ultimately, its value depends upon its usefulness, on its ability to perform the function for which it was built and designed. The same is true of many other objects we possess: washing machines, mobile telephones, laptop computers, garden tools. If they do not work, they have little or no value.

The kingdom of heaven is not like this. If we meet it we experience something that is of no use to us. Its value resides in itself. However, it may affect us in different ways. It may make us forget completely about ourselves, about the anxieties that we have at present, or the ambitions that are dominating our lives. It may suddenly relate us to other people in ways that are entirely unselfish and which are governed only by generosity. It may make us feel strangers to ourselves and strangers in the world in which we live. It may set off in our minds searching questions about who we are and what our purpose in the world is.

---

[4] M.Luther, Großer Katechismus, in *Die Bekenntnisschriften der evangelisch-lutherischen Kirche*, Göttingen: Vandenhoeck & Ruprecht, 1979, pp. 673-4.

Suppose we see a beautiful sunset. This can be a deeply moving experience. It is of no practical use to us and its beauty resides in itself. Yet we may be so moved by what we see that we want to tell someone else so that they can see it also. Our motive in doing this is entirely self-less. We do not do it because we want to show that we are more knowledgeable than the person to whom we speak. It is not on our part an exercise of power over another person. It comes from a sincere desire that someone else should experience the beauty, awe and wonder which we have found so moving.

This brings me to the main and central point of this evening's lecture. Towards the end of his book, published in 1919, Clutton-Brock describes an occasion in his childhood on which he says he was offered the kingdom of heaven and refused it. He writes as follows

> I was lagging behind my nurse on a walk in my own native west country in spring, when three children ran out of a cottage garden, holding in their hands small branches of sycamore from which they had stripped all but the young bronze-coloured leaves at the top. These branches they offered to me; I can still see them offering them as if they were performing a rite and they smiled as they offered them. But I looked at them and ran after my nurse without saying a word; and, when I turned back to look at them again, they were still standing in the road holding the branches out as if they had been disappointed. I had disappointed them; and for days afterwards I kept thinking of them standing so; and even then I wondered why they seemed to me so pitiful and myself so mean. As I explain it now, the kingdom of heaven was offered to me then in the road, and I refused it.[5]

Of course, Clutton-Brock did not refuse the kingdom of heaven. What he refused was the totally unselfish and

---

[5] Clutton-Brock, *Kingdom of Heaven*, pp. 118-9.

instinctive act of love and generosity on the part of three small children, and we must remember that children can be as cruel to each other as adults are. But the act of love and generosity on the part of the three children hinted at and in some way expressed the kingdom of heaven. It expressed a realm of right relationships, a dimension of beauty, purity, and loveliness.

At this point I want to return to the matter of the two phrases 'kingdom of heaven' and 'kingdom of God'. The reason why we have the two phrases is that 'kingdom of God' is found in the Gospel of Mark, and that 'kingdom of heaven' is what we have in Matthew. It is usually said, correctly, that Matthew's use of 'heaven' is an example of the Jewish reverence for God, which means that instead of saying 'God' another word, such as 'heaven', is used instead. For the writer of Matthew's Gospel then, the word 'heaven' was a way of being respectful to God. For our purposes the importance of the phrase 'kingdom of heaven' is that it enables us to talk about the kingdom in a non-religious way. The act of offering sycamore branches to Clutton-Brock was not a religious action in the sense that it was done in the context of a religious ceremony or religious beliefs. However, if it was not religious in a narrow technical sense, it was certainly spiritual, and I want to develop this idea at some length.

Clutton-Brock published 'What is the Kingdom of Heaven?' in 1919. Only two years earlier, in 1917, the German theologian Rudolf Otto had published his book 'The Idea of the Holy', a work that has had a profound influence upon the study of religion in general.[6] Otto described and analysed human experiences in which there was an encounter with what Otto variously called 'the holy', 'the wholly other', and the

---

[6] R. Otto, *Das Heilige. Über das Irrationale in der Idee des Göttlichen und sein Verhältnis zum Rationalen*, Munich: C. H. Beck, 1917, ET *The Idea of the Holy. An Inquiry into the Non-rational Factor in the Idea of the Divine and its relations to the Rational*, Harmondsworth: Penguin, 1959.

'numinous'. In each case the result of such an encounter was to make a person aware of being confronted by something that was so much more real than his own being, something that could fill him with awe and wonder. In the example given by Clutton-Brock, his refusal of the gift offered made him feel mean. One of the examples used by Otto is from Isaiah chapter six, where the prophet sees in a vision the exalted Lord, and exclaims in awe and wonder 'Woe is me for I am undone, for mine eyes have seen the Lord of hosts, the King'. This, of course, is a description of a religious experience. However, in a follow-up book published in 1923, Otto drew attention to experiences of the numinous or the holy which were not necessarily religious, but which were certainly spiritual, and I want to say something about several examples now.

In John Ruskin's essay 'Of many things', Ruskin describes how he felt moved by his encounters with nature as a young man. The quotation is as follows:

> although there was no definite religious sentiment mingled with it, there was a continual perception of sanctity in the whole of nature, from the slightest thing to the vastest; an instinctive awe, mixed with delight; an indefinable thrill, such as we sometimes imagine to indicate the presence of a disembodied spirit. I could only feel this perfectly when I was alone, and then it would often make me shiver from head to foot with the joy and fear of it, when after being some time away from hills, I first got to the shore of a mountain river, where the brown water circled among the pebbles, or when I first saw the swell of distant land against the sunset, or the first low broken wall, covered with mountain moss. I cannot in the least describe the feeling; but I do not think this is my fault, nor that of the English language, for I am afraid, no feeling is describable. If we had to explain even the sense of bodily hunger to a person who had never felt it, we should be hard put to it for words; and the joy in nature seemed to me to come of a sort of heart-hunger, satisfied with the presence of a Great and Holy Spirit.[7]

Those of you who remember my aversion to the hymn 'All things bright and beautiful' may be surprised to hear me quoting this from Ruskin. Isn't Ruskin advocating 'All things bright and beautiful' it may be asked? Definitely not! There is all the difference in the world between trying to prove the existence of God by arguing from the beauty of nature (and ignoring its malevolent parts), and being confronted by the holy, or whatever you want to call it, in nature, so that, to quote Ruskin, 'one shivers from head to foot with the joy and fear of it'. The most significant phrase in Ruskin's words is when he speaks of 'a sort of heart-hunger' – which we might interpret as a feeling of incompleteness, of being away from home, of feeling as if in a strange land – yet an experience that suggests that there is something that can satisfy the heart-hunger, can make us feel that there is a home or land to which we rightly belong.

Such experiences, I contend, are experiences of the kingdom of heaven and they are more common than we might suppose. Paul Tillich relates an experience that he had in the Kaiser-Wilhelm Museum in Berlin shortly after he returned from military duty as an army chaplain in the First World War.

> I stood in front of one of the pictures of the Madonna by Botticelli. In a moment that I can only describe as inspiration, there opened to me the sense of what a painting can reveal. It can disclose a new dimension of being, but only when it also has the power to open a corresponding window in the soul. It was only natural for a theologian to ask how this inspiration related to what theology calls inspiration. How does aesthetic experience relate to the religious function of the human spirit?[8]

---

[7] J. Ruskin, 'Of Many Things', in *Modern Painters*, vol. 3, London: George Allen, 1906, p. 309, quoted in R. Otto, *Aufsätze, das Numinose betreffend*, Stuttgart/Gotha, Verlag Friedrich Andreas Perthes, 1923, pp. 56-7.
[8] W. Schüssler, E. Sturm, *Paul Tillich. Leben- Werk –Wirkung*, Darmstadt: Wissenschaftliche Buchgesellschaft, 2007, pp. 65-6 (my translation).

My former colleague and onetime teacher John Heywood Thomas has summarised Tillich's view in the following words:

> Revelation [for Tillich] is the occurrence of an event which evokes "numinous astonishment", by which term he means the feeling of being in the grip of a mystery, yet elated with awe...The occurrence of this whole situation is revelation. The vehicle of revelation is an experience which is charged with the sense of the mystery of existence. The sign event may be historical happenings, happenings in nature, or in the lives of saints "whose faith and love can become sign events for those who are grasped by their power of creativity".[9]

In C. S. Lewis's 'The Pilgrim's Regress', its hero, John, has a vision of an island, which sets him on his long quest for hope and certainty, and ultimately, Christianity. He finds himself one day

> so far away from home that he was in a part of the road he had never seen before. Then came the sound of a musical instrument, from behind, it seemed, very sweet and very short, as if one were plucking of a string or one note of a bell, and after it a full, clear voice – and it sounded so high and strange he thought it was very far away, further than a star. The voice said, Come. Then John saw that there was a stone wall beside the road in that part: but it had (what he had never seen in a garden wall before) a window. There was no glass in the window and no bars; it was just a square hole in the wall. Through it he saw a green wood full of primroses...while he strained to grasp it, there came to him from beyond the wood a sweetness and a pang so piercing that he forgot his father's house and his mother...A moment later he found he was sobbing. And the sun had gone in...it seemed to him that a mist which hung at the far end of the wood had parted for a moment, and through the rift he had

---

[9] J. H. Thomas, *Paul Tillich. An Appraisal*, London: SCM Press, 1963, p. 50.

seen a calm sea, and in the sea an island, where the smooth turf sloped down unbroken to the bays...He had no inclination yet to go into the wood· and presently he went home with a sad excitement upon him, repeating to himself a thousand times, "I know now what I want".[10]

In their biography of C. S. Lewis, Roger Lancelot Green and Walter Hooper accept that 'The Pilgrim's Regress' provides autobiographical information about Lewis's journey into Christian faith.[11] So it may well be that Lewis is using the person of John to describe an experience that he once had. Even if it is not autobiographical, it is a vivid description of a frequent kind of spiritual experience that sets people on a quest for ultimate meaning for their lives.

The Canadian political philosopher, Charles Taylor, uses the word 'epiphany' to describe art, literature and poetry as expressions of a creative imagination that 'reveals...[and] at the same time defines and completes what it makes manifest'. 'What I want to capture with this term [epiphany]' he writes, 'is just this notion of a work of art as the locus of a manifestation which brings us into the presence of something which is otherwise inaccessible, and which is of the highest moral and spiritual significance; a manifestation, moreover, which also defines or completes something, even as it reveals'.[12]

Finally in this section I want to return to Rudolf Otto's 1923 book in which he collects accounts of experiences of the 'holy' or whatever we want to call it. The examples include excerpts from St. Augustine's 'Confessions', from Martin Luther and significantly, from Buddhist and Hindu writings and art. The

[10] C. S. Lewis, *The Pilgrim's Regress, An Allegorical Apology for Christianity, Reason and Romanticism*, London: HarperCollins, 1998, pp. 8-9.
[11] R. L. Green, W. Hooper, *C. S. Lewis. A Biography*, London: Collins, 1974, p. 9.
[12] C. Taylor, *Sources of the Self. The Making of the Modern Identity*, Cambridge: Cambridge University Press, 1989, p. 419.

importance of these latter examples, from eastern mystical experience, is that it shows we are dealing with something which reaches far beyond the Jewish-Christian tradition into the experience of humanity as a whole.

The importance of this is that it shows that what I am calling 'the kingdom of heaven' as opposed for the moment to 'the kingdom of God' is an indication that we humans are spiritual beings, not in the sense that we are capable of generating spiritual feelings within ourselves, but in the sense that in the world in which we live there is a spiritual dimension or world which is independent of us; a world of harmony and beauty, of right relationships, a world that we may meet from time to time in awe-inspiring moments which move us to ask searching questions about who and what we are. For much of the time humans are ignorant of this spiritual dimension, or explain it away in psychological language, and organise their lives and the world with such business and such concentration upon technological gadgetry that they become one-dimensional beings. But they are not one-dimensional, and the spiritual experiences of people over vast stretches of time and space provide evidence for the fact that there is a spiritual dimension independent of us, which is as real a part of our world as the objects of the physical universe.

The realisation of this is important for the church's task. The remainder of these lectures will deal with the kingdom of God, that is, the kingdom of heaven as revealed in the Bible and the mission of Jesus; but the fact of the kingdom of heaven, a spiritual dimension that is part of our world and capable of being experienced by the humanity of any culture or belief-system, means that when the Gospel is preached we should feel that we are knocking on doors that may be shut, but which are not locked; that God goes before us and reaches out to humanity in his own ways.

If this sounds un-Christian and too inter-faith in the modern sense, we must remind ourselves of Acts 17. Paul, you will remember, comes to Athens, where he sees an altar dedicated TO THE UNKNOWN GOD and addressing the philosophers and others who gather to hear him he says

> Whom ...ye ignorantly worship, him declare I unto you. God...hath made of one blood all nations of men for to dwell on all the face of the earth, and hath determined the times beforehand appointed, and the bounds of their habitation; That they should seek the Lord, if haply they might feel after him and find him, though he be not far from every one of us; For in him we live, and move, and have our being; as certain also of your own poets have said, For we are also his offspring.

It is noteworthy that Paul refers to a Greek poet, probably Aratus, who was active in Athens in the early 3rd century BC, and allows that independently of the Jewish/Christian revelation, God has made it possible for men to seek after him and find him, although Paul now wishes to declare to his listeners that what they have groped after uncertainly, God has declared openly in Jesus Christ.

In his 'Readings in St. John's Gospel', Archbishop William Temple comments as follows on the phrase in the Prologue to that Gospel 'That was the true Light, which lighteth every man that cometh into the world' (John 1.9).

> By the Word of God – that is to say, by Jesus Christ – Isaiah, and Plato, and Zoroaster, and Buddha, and Confucius conceived and uttered such truths as they declared. There is only one divine light; and every man in his measure is enlightened by it.[13]

---

[13] W. Temple, *Readings in St. John's Gospel*, London: Macmillan, 1952, p. 10.

'There is only one divine light; and every man in his measure is enlightened by it.' This does not mean that all religions are the same (patently they are not!), and that it doesn't matter what people believe. Paul and Archbishop Temple would have been scandalised by this conclusion, not to mention the writer of the opening chapter of John's Gospel who proclaims that 'the Word was made flesh and dwelt among us'. But it does put into a wider perspective what we think about the kingdom of God, and its relation to the religious experience of mankind. The kingdom of God as revealed in the Bible is a particular and special instance of that spiritual world or dimension which is part of God's creation and through which his divine light has and does enlighten those who are open to it. It is important that we never forget this, and that we resist all attempts to explain and understand our world and our humanity purely in terms of scientific and technological concepts.

There is one final matter to be considered, and that concerns the term 'kingdom'. In English a kingdom is a piece of territory, within which people live. We live in the United Kingdom of Great Britain and Northern Ireland. When Jesus spoke of the kingdom of God he used the Aramaic word *mal^ekhutā* which was translated into Greek as *basileia* in the Gospels. Both *mal^ekhutā* and *basileia* have the sense of 'king**ship**' rather than 'king**dom**' and when James Moffatt translated the New Testament in the early part of the last century he translated *basileia* as 'reign' rather than 'kingdom'. Thus, Mark 1.14-15 reads in the Moffatt translation:

> After John had been arrested, Jesus went to Galilee preaching the gospel of God; he said, 'The time has now come, God's reign is near: repent and believe the gospel'.

Another translation option would be 'the rule of God'. I was surprised when looking through the modern translations that I possess that none of them apart from Moffatt seemed to have addressed the matter of what exactly Jesus meant by *mal^{e}khutā*. However, for the purposes of these lectures I shall stay with 'kingdom'.

Before I conclude I shall try to answer a question which may be in the minds of some of you. If the kingdom of God was so central to the preaching and teaching of Jesus, why was Clutton-Brock's inquirer unable to find any reference to it in the creeds and in the formularies of the Church of England? The answer is that the creeds were never intended to be complete statements of Christian belief, but rather to emphasise the central importance of Jesus Christ in the revelation of God. They say nothing about the Bible, or the Sacraments, or about justification by faith. It is unfortunate, in a way, that they have often been thought of as if they were complete statements of Christian belief! The matter of the formularies is more complicated, but the simple answer is that over the centuries the Church came to believe that it was the kingdom of God on earth, and that one of its main tasks was to facilitate the salvation of individual men and women. At the Reformation there was disagreement among Catholics and Protestants about the nature and composition of the church and of the way of salvation, and these matters became central to the 39 Articles. However, it is regrettable that they omitted all reference to the kingdom of God.

I hope that we have made better progress this evening, and that you will join me as we continue our pursuit of this topic during the remainder of Lent. Next week's lecture deals with the kingship of God in the Old Testament.

LECTURE 2

The Kingship of God
in the Old Testament

One of the surprising things about today's world is the attention that we pay to our leaders, and the hopes that we invest in them. Who is going to be the new prime minister of Italy, or Spain, or Greece? ask the newspapers and news programmes. Who will be the next leader of the Liberal Democrats? Who will be the next British prime minister? With a change of government and leader come new hopes for the future. Certainly, the leaders themselves try to give the impression, especially when in opposition, that if they come to power they will radically improve the condition of the country. If we, in today's world, place such hopes in our political leaders, it should come as no surprise that in the ancient world similar hopes were placed in kings and rulers to the extent that some of them were considered to be divine, or claimed themselves to be divine.

In 1948 Henri Frankfort published a massive study of the ideas of kingship in the ancient world under the title 'Kingship and the Gods'.[14] This was a survey of material from ancient Egypt and Mesopotamia, covering all aspects of kingship, and how kings were believed to integrate society and the natural world into one sacred whole. An epilogue entitled 'The Hebrews' shrewdly observed some fundamental differences between the ancient Israelite concept of kingship and that which obtained in the ancient Near East to the point where Frankfort wrote that kingship for the Hebrews 'has no place in a "study of ancient Near Eastern religion as an integration of society and nature"'.[15] However, this did not prevent Old Testament scholars from using material from the ancient Near East to reconstruct rituals that were said to have taken place in the temple in Jerusalem, and in which the king played a central role. Psalm 2, in particular, was said to be a coronation psalm in which, at a crucial point in the ceremony, the king was handed a scroll by a priest or other official, in which he read his mandate from God: 'thou art my son; this day have I begotten thee'. This meant that the king had become the adopted son of the God of Israel, and stood in a special position, mediating between the people and God, and ensuring that God's just rule was exercised over the people.

It would be easy to conclude from this that when the writers of the Old Testament spoke of the kingship of God, they were merely projecting human ideas of rulership on to a divine being, who was created more or less in the human image. The remarkable thing about the Old Testament, in fact, is that it came to regard all its kings as fundamentally flawed human beings, who could certainly not serve as pointers to God's kingship, and whose failures only generated longings for an

---

[14] H. Frankfort, *Kingship and the Gods. A Study of Ancient Near Eastern Religion as the Integration of Society & Nature*, Chicago: University of Chicago Press, 1948.
[15] Frankfort, *Kingship*, p. 344.

ideal divine rule, and an ideal kingdom whose achievement was beyond the capacity of the human race. This is clearly demonstrated by the person of the greatest king in the Old Testament, David!

In 1 Samuel 13.14 David is described as a man after God's own heart, and in various parts of the Old Testament there is the hope of the coming of a reborn David to rule his people. Yet in 2 Samuel chapters 11 to 20 David is spared nothing as the story is told of how he committed adultery with Bathsheba, the wife of one of his soldiers, Uriah, who was on the battle field, and made her pregnant; how he recalled that soldier back to Jerusalem in the hope that he would sleep with his wife so that the child in her womb would be thought to be his and not David's; how, when Uriah declined to sleep with his wife, David sent him back to the scene of the battle, with instructions to his commander in chief to place Uriah in the front line of battle so that he would be killed. When David heard the news of Uriah's death he sent for Bathsheba and took her into his household. At this point, Nathan the prophet comes to David to denounce his behaviour in the name of God, and David repents. Yet this is only the beginning of David's troubles. His son Amnon rapes a half-sister named Tamar, and Tamar's full brother Absalom, revenges Tamar by having Amnon killed. Absalom next leads a rebellion against David, which succeeds to the point that David has to flee from Jerusalem and take refuge across the Jordan, where Absalom is killed after he gets entangled in a great oak tree. There is then another rebellion, led this time by a disaffected member of the family of Saul, David's predecessor as king. In the closing chapter of 2 Samuel, chapter 24, David holds a census of the people, an act which he then believes to be a sin. In order to pay for that sin, a prophet, Gad, offers David three choices: that there should be three years of famine, or that he should flee from his enemies for three months, or that a pestilence should ravage his people for three days. David chooses the pestilence and seventy thousand people die.

This is not a flattering picture of an ideal king, a man after God's own heart, and the pattern for a future hoped-for ruler! For centuries the church tried to avoid the implications of the biblical picture of David by distinguishing between what he did as a private person, which was dubious, and what he did in his office as a king, which was perfect. But this strategy could not hold out for ever, and in 1697 Pierre Bayle published an article on David in his great 'Dictionary' which did not hesitate to rehearse David's faults critically, on the grounds that they were publicly recorded in the Bible for any reader to see. [16] In fact, the church had misunderstood the intentions of the biblical writers. The biblical writers were under no compulsion to record David's misdeeds, and presumably could easily have omitted them if they had really wanted to present David only as a paragon of virtue. That they portrayed David warts and all, as we would say, was for a reason, and that reason was to indicate that the 'man after God's own heart' was a flawed human being whose life could not be projected into the divine sphere so as to express the kingship of God. The biblical writers were saying 'put not your trust in princes, nor in any child of man, for there is no hope in them' to quote Psalm 146.3.

This critical view of David and his flaws was carried over into the editing of the book of Psalms and the titles that were added to them. The tradition that David composed many of the psalms was part of this appraisal of him, where, when we read the psalms attributed to David, we get a picture of a humble man of faith, surrounded by his enemies and beset by personal difficulties which make him call upon God for

---

[16] P. Bayle, *A General Dictionary, Historical and Critical*, (trans. J. P. Bernard, et al.), London, 1736, vol. IV, pp. 532-42.

deliverance. Most famously, the title of Psalm 51, that most eloquent psalm of contrition and prayer for God's forgiveness, is linked with David's sin after he has committed adultery with Bathsheba.

This portrayal of David in the psalms as the humble man in need of God's mercy, as opposed to him being some kind of superman who is the pattern for the kingship of God, opens the way for a new interpretation of the psalms of the kingship of God. I want to illustrate this from the most recent research on Psalm 2.[17]

I said above that it is possible to find in this psalm traces of an ancient coronation ritual in which the king is declared to be the son of God, that is, to be admitted to an office that carries particular responsibility for governing justly and wisely. However, in its present form the psalm is concerned with the universal rule of God over all the nations. Zion and Jerusalem have a special place in this, but this is because it is Zion's and Jerusalem's God who is the lord of the earth and its inhabitants.

The psalm begins with an account of rebellion by the nations against God and his anointed king:

> Why do the nations conspire,
> And the peoples plot in vain?
> The kings of the earth set themselves,
> And the rulers take counsel together,
> Against the LORD and his anointed, saying
> 'Let us burst their bonds asunder,
> And cast their cords from us'.

---

[17] See M. Saur, *Die Königspsalmen. Studien zur Entstehung und Theologie*, (Beihefte zur Zeitschrift für die alttestamentliche Wissenschaft 340), Berlin: W. De Gruyter, 2004, pp. 25-46; F. Hartenstein, B. Janowski, *Psalmen* (Biblischer Kommentar Altes Testament XV/1), Neukirchen-Vluyn: Neukirchener Verlag, 2012, pp. 55-80.

The older commentaries get into a real tangle trying to suggest a time in Israel's history when Israel had control of an empire whose subject nations wished to throw off the yoke of subjection.[18] There never was such a time. What is envisaged here is the desire of humanity, as represented by the nations, to refuse to be subject to God's kingship.

The futility of trying to deny the ultimate assertion of God's sovereignty is now stated.

> He who sits in the heavens laughs;
> The LORD has them in derision.
> Then he will speak to them in his wrath,
> And terrify them in his fury.
> 'I have set my king on Zion, my holy hill'.

The next part of the psalm probably incorporates material from an ancient coronation ceremony in which the king is admitted to his office and is promised victory over his enemies. In the psalm's present form, this means that God's purposes revealed through his people Israel and represented by the king will ultimately triumph.

> I will tell of the decree of the LORD:
> He said to me 'You are my son,
> Today I have begotten you.
> Ask of me, and I will make the nations your heritage,
> And the ends of the earth your possession.
> You shall break them with a rod of iron,
> and dash them in pieces like a potter's vessel'.

The two final verses are addressed to the nations of the earth.

> Now therefore, O kings, be wise;

---

[18] See the otherwise generally excellent commentary of A. F. Kirkpatrick, *The Book of Psalms*, Cambridge: Cambridge University Press, vol. 1, 1930, pp. 5-8.

Be warned, O rulers of the earth.
Serve the LORD with fear,
With trembling kiss his feet,
Lest he be angry, and you perish in the way;
For his wrath is quickly kindled.
Blessed are all those who take refuge in him.

This psalm claims, then, that the God of what by any standards in the ancient world was a tiny, culturally backward and politically insignificant nation, is the de facto ruler of the world and its peoples, that his purposes have been disclosed to this insignificant people, and that his rule will one day be seen to be established in the world. [19] This insight comes from complete disillusionment with earthly rulers and a willingness to present the country's most illustrious king as flawed and immoral.

A similar transformation of ideas is seen in another strand of tradition in the Old Testament, that of the day of the LORD. The Old Testament is full of stories in which the God of Israel acts on behalf of his people to defeat their enemies. At the crossing of the Red Sea God destroys the armies of the Egyptians, allowing the Hebrews to escape. In Judges 5, a hymn that celebrates an Israelite victory over a coalition of Canaanite kings, God is said to have swept Israel's enemies away by releasing a cloudburst on to the plain of Jezreel which bogged down the chariots of the enemy. How far the cultural memory of the people had embellished these events, we do not know, but it is likely that the cultural memory probably remembered these things rather in the way that we remember the Battle of Britain and the Spanish Armada, and exaggerate the odds against us.

---

[19] It is interesting that in the New Testament the psalm is quoted in Acts 4.25-8 and seen to refer to the rejection of God's anointed, i.e. Jesus, by Herod and Pontius Pilate, and the Gentiles and the people of Israel.. Kirkpatrick, *Psalms*, p. 7 lists other references to Psalm 2 in the New Testament.

It seems that in popular thought, therefore, the day of the LORD was thought of as a time when God would act mightily on behalf of Israel and against her enemies. It must therefore have been a great shock when the people heard the following words from the prophet Amos around the year 740 BC.

> Woe to you who desire the day of the LORD!
> Why would you have the day of the LORD?
> It is darkness and not light;
> As if a man fled from a lion,
> And a bear met him;
> Or went into the home and leaned with his hand against the wall,
> And a serpent bit him.
> Is not the day of the LORD darkness, and not light.,
> And gloom with no brightness in it? (Amos 5.19-20)

The idea that prophets, whose job it was to say good things about the nation and its rulers, should speak against the nation and threaten it with judgement from the God that was supposed to be its protector, was not very welcome, as we can imagine; and Amos became the first of a line of prophets of judgement, some of whom suffered abuse and threats against their life. They included Micah in the 8th century, and Jeremiah and Ezekiel in the 6th century.

One of the most remarkable descriptions of the day of the LORD is found in Isaiah 2.12-22

> For the LORD of hosts has a day
> against all that is proud and lofty,
> against all that is lifted up and high,
> against all the cedars of Lebanon,
> lofty and lifted up,
> and against all the oaks of Bashan;
> against all the high mountains
> and against all the lofty hills;
> against every high tower,

and against every fortified wall;
against all the ships of Tarshish,
and against all the beautiful craft
And the haughtiness of man shall be humbled,
and the pride of men shall be brought low;
and the LORD alone will be exalted in that day.
And the idols shall utterly pass away.
And men shall enter the caves of the rocks
and the holes of the ground,
from before the terror of the LORD,
and from the glory of his majesty,
when he rises to terrify the earth.
In that day men will cast forth
their idols of silver and their idols of gold,
which they made for themselves to worship,
to the moles and to the bats,
to enter the caverns of the rocks
and the clefts of the cliffs,
from before the terror of the LORD,
and from the glory of his majesty,
when he rises to terrify the earth.
Turn away from man
in whose nostrils is breath,
for of what account is he?

In this passage the majesty of God is directed against all manifestations of human pride and pomp. The cedars of Lebanon and the oaks of Bashan were the mighty trees that made possible the building of palaces and temples. The ships of Tarshish were the blue riband trading ships that enabled precious metals and rare spices to be bought and sold by the rich and powerful. The lofty hills, high towers and fortified walls were the fortified cities which protected the rich and powerful and from which they ruled. The idols of silver and gold represented the religion of human self-sufficiency, worshipping the fruits of human achievement. While none of them were wrong in themselves, they tended towards a one-dimensional view of the self-sufficiency of the human race, with religion and the gods only recognised to the extent that they served human needs and made no moral demands. The prophetic message was a warning against such self-satisfaction and was particularly apt at times when natural disasters such as earthquakes disclosed how fragile the human domination of the natural world was. It is a message that we still need to heed as we wonder why houses built in flood plains or earthquake zones do not afford permanent and unshakeable protection to those who live in them.

Yet the prophetic message of the kingship of God as expressed in the concept of the day of the LORD is not all gloom and doom. The book of Joel, which is dominated by the concept of the day of the LORD, sees the divine judgement as the prelude to divine blessing. The promise of blessing that follows the warnings of judgement ends with the famous passage about the outpouring of God's spirit.

> And it shall come to pass afterward,
> that I will pour out my spirit on all flesh;
> your sons and your daughters shall prophesy,
> your old men shall dream dreams
> and your young men shall see visions.
> Even upon the menservants and maidservants
> in those days, I will pour out my spirit.
>
> *(Joel 2.28-9, Hebrew 3.1-2)*

This means that a reversal of the material fortunes of the people will be accompanied by spiritual blessings, which will put into a new context the material conditions of the people. They will see their material blessings as divine gifts. They will not be tempted to practise that human pride and self-sufficiency that are so comforting for the powerful, but a curse to those who are the means to the power of the powerful. The benefits of God's kingship will be available to all.

Another remarkable witness to the kingship of God in the Old Testament is found in a group of psalms from Psalm 93 to 99.

Several of them begin with the acclamation 'The LORD is king' according to the older translations, or 'The LORD reigns' in the Revised Standard Version. An important emphasis in these psalms is that of social justice, as the deeds of the inhumane rulers are described.

> They pour out their arrogant words,
> they boast, all the evildoers.
> They crush thy people, O LORD,
> and afflict thy heritage.
> They slay the widow and the sojourner,
> and murder the fatherless;
> and they say, 'the LORD does not see;
> the God of Jacob does not perceive'. (Psalm 94.4-7)

This same psalm (94) also condemns the arrogant corruption of rulers who pass unjust laws in order to lend legality and respectability to their wickedness.

> Can wicked rulers be allied with thee,
> who frame mischief by statute? (Psalm 94.20)

Or, as I have translated this line in my book 'The Psalms in Daily Life'

> Can those who cover up their wickedness have you as an ally,
> Those who produce evil by passing laws?[20]

Yet the part of these psalms that always impresses me most is where the coming judgement of God is seen as a blessing to the world of nature.

> Let the heavens be glad, and let the earth rejoice;
> let the sea roar, and all that fills it;
> let the field exult, and everything in it!
> Then shall all the trees of the wood sing for joy

---

[20] J. W. Rogerson, *The Psalms in Daily Life*, London: SPCK, 2001, p. 38.

before the LORD, for he comes,
for he comes to judge the earth.
He will judge the world with righteousness,
and the peoples with his truth. (Psalm 96. 11-13)

Judgement here is good news! It is good news because it is God's righteous judgement, a judgement that will deliver the world from human cruelty to other humans, and human cruelty to the world of nature. The day of the Lord will be bad news only to those who want to live in God's world without acknowledging that it *is* God's world; to those who have no regard to what is right and wrong and who treat their fellow human beings accordingly. It has been said that the anger of God in the Old Testament is not directed at the human race, but at those things that harm and disfigure the human race.[21]

The strongest vision of the kingship of God as expressed in Old Testament hopes for a better world comes in the well-known passage in Micah 4.1-4, which is also repeated in Isaiah 2.2-4.

It shall come to pass in the latter days
that the mountain of the house of the LORD
Shall be established as the highest of the mountains,
and shall be raised up above the hills;
and peoples shall flow to it,
and many nations shall come, and say,
'Come, let us go up to the mountain of the LORD,
to the house of the God of Jacob;
that he may teach us his ways
and we may go in his paths.
For out of Zion shall go forth the law,
and the word of the LORD from Jerusalem.
He shall judge between many peoples,

---

[21] W.Dietrich, C. Link, *Die dunklen Seiten Gottes. Band 2, Allmacht und Ohnmacht,* Neukirchen-Vluyn: Neukirchener Verlag, 2000, p. 323, and see the whole section on the day of the Lord, pp. 322-330.

and shall decide for strong nations afar off;
and they shall beat their swords into ploughshares,
and their spears into pruning hooks;
nation shall not lift up sword against nation,
neither shall they learn war any more;
but they shall sit every man under his vine and under his fig
tree,
and none shall make them afraid;
For the mouth of the LORD of hosts has spoken.

It is interesting to compare this vision with the material in Psalm 2 that had been taken over from an ancient Israelite coronation ceremony. In Psalm 2, that material envisages that Zion's king will crush his enemies and break them in pieces. In the Micah vision it is the nations themselves that will break in pieces their instruments of war. They will not band together against God, as in Psalm 2. They will go willingly to Zion in order to hear the word of God and to learn his ways. The theme of the kingship of God has gained more depth and breadth.

Before I end I want to mention a complicated matter that will become crucial in the next two lectures. The texts that I have quoted refer to the future; but what is the future? We have to reckon with the fact that although time is measured scientifically, it is constructed and experienced socially. It was after all the invention of railways in the 19th century that made it necessary for Britain and other countries to adopt national and international standards of time, as opposed to the previous local standards, where the real time for a community was what the clock on the local church tower said it was. What was it like to live at a time and in a society where there were no clocks, no methods of time reckoning in terms of BC and AD, no long-term planning? In his book 'Yesterday, Today and Tomorrow. Time and History in the Old Testament', Simon DeVries argues that

The Hebrews were so intensely interested in the future because they knew they had a share in shaping it; also because they believed their God was waiting on their action...Always the future that awaited them was predicted in terms that were calculated to influence their present behaviour. If it was to be a day of woe, it was designed to move them to repentance and conversion; if it was to be a day of bliss, it was designed to move them out of despair. Thus Israel's concern with the future was, if anything, eminently practical and personalistic. It involved the personhood of God and the personhood of man in free interaction, both of which were guaranteed because the future was not predetermined but open to the loving, trusting partnership of God as history's purposeful shaper and man as history's responsible actor.[22]

In this quotation I do not like the phrases 'the Hebrews' and 'Israel' as though what is being said applied to every Israelite without exception. What DeVries says is true of certain Israelites, most notably the prophets, and that is all that matters for our purposes. The point is that when we read texts such as Micah 4, we should not think of them as referring to a future Golden Age that may never be realised in our world. We must see them as visions that both judge and inspire us in the present, and which give us the hope that, in our openness to God and with his help, the future can be altered for the better.

In the Old Testament, the kingship of God is not the arbitrary rule of a dictator who forces through his programmes against the will of the people he governs. The kingship of God is designed to move human hearts and wills to do what they see to be best for the human race and the world that it inhabits.

---

[22] S. J. DeVries, *Yesterday, Today and Tomorrow. Time and History in the Old Testament*, London: SPCK, 1975, p. 282.

LECTURE 3

The Kingdom of God in the Teaching of Jesus

'Now after John was arrested, Jesus came into Galilee, preaching the gospel of God, and saying, "The time is fulfilled, and the kingdom of God is at hand; repent, and believe in the gospel"' (Mark 1.14-15).

Mark's summary of the preaching of Jesus, centred on the kingdom of God, is amplified in the remainder of his Gospel. At a rough estimate, Mark has 19 references to the kingdom of God in the teaching of Jesus, while in the material common to Matthew and Luke and not found in Mark, there are roughly 30 references to the kingdom in the teaching of Jesus. However, the kingdom is at the heart of all that Jesus said, whether or not he explicitly mentioned the kingdom of God.

To try to explain what he meant by the phrase, I must begin, as Mark does, with John the Baptist, and the proclamation of Jesus that the kingdom of God is 'at hand'. John stood in the line of succession of the prophets of the Old Testament and although he did not used the phrase 'day of the Lord' (one of the subjects of last week's lecture), his use of Isaiah 40.3-5 –

'Prepare the way of the Lord, make his paths straight, Every valley shall be filled, and every mountain and hill shall be brought low' had resonances with day of the Lord passages elsewhere in the prophetic books. The idea of mountains and hills being brought low resonates strongly with Isaiah 2 where the Lord will be lifted up against high hills and lofty towers on his day. For John, the day of the Lord was so close to coming that he exhorted people to be baptised, as an indication that they wished to be associated no longer with the lives which they had lived up to now, but with the coming age in which all flesh would see the salvation of God. As in the prophecies of the day of the Lord in the Old Testament, this coming age would involve judgement upon the present age. 'Even now the axe is laid to the root of the trees; every tree therefore that does not bear good fruit is cut down and thrown into the fire' (Matthew 3.9) The background, then, to Jesus's preaching of the kingdom of God were the expectations raised by John's preaching that the day of the Lord was very close at hand.

What did Jesus mean when he said that kingdom of God was 'at hand'? The translation 'is at hand' goes back to William Tyndale, and was used by all the main English translations until the New English Bible rendered the Greek as 'is upon you', although J. B. Phillips had earlier tried 'has arrived'. The New International Version prefers 'is near'. It will be clear from these attempts that it is not easy to translate the Greek, although Jesus had spoken Aramaic, of course. The Greek tense used is the perfect tense, which means that something has happened in the past which is now affecting the present. J. B. Phillips's 'has arrived' gets closer to this than any other translation of the ones I have mentioned, but it needs to be elaborated.

If I order a taxi and my wife tells me that it has arrived, she is indeed referring to something that has happened in the past and is affecting the present. She is not saying that it is 'at hand' or that it 'is near'. She is saying that it is there outside the front door, that it is available for me to use, and that I must make the decision to get into it if I want to go to the place for which I ordered it. This is close to what Jesus meant when he said that the kingdom of God had drawn near (to translate the Greek literally). The kingdom was not about to come, it was not just around the corner. It had arrived as certainly as my taxi had arrived. However, while it is obvious when a taxi arrives, the arrival of the kingdom of God was hidden, to some extent. Or, to put it another way, it could be seen if you knew what to look for, but not seen if you were looking for something else. This last point affected even John the Baptist. 'Are you really the one who is to come, or should we look for someone else?' he sent messengers to ask Jesus (Matthew 11.3). John evidently expected the day of the Lord to consist of mighty supernatural demonstrations of the power of God. Because he was looking for the wrong thing, he could not see the kingdom of God; and the same was true of those opponents of Jesus who could not understand how an apparently uneducated craftsman from Nazareth, one who, moreover, seemed not to realise that he was breaking the commandments of God by not observing the Sabbath in the proper way, could by any stretch of the imagination be the Chosen One whose coming into the world was part of the coming of the kingdom of God into the world. So, what was the kingdom of God that Jesus proclaimed like? I shall try to answer this question under three headings: the kingdom as a kind of sacred space, the kingdom as a dimension whose logic confounds normal human logic, and the kingdom as something that resonates deeply with human emotions and aspirations.

The Kingdom of God as a kind of sacred space

I said in the first lecture that the Greek word *basileia* meant king**ship** rather than king**dom** and I shall continue to maintain this. The kingdom of God is not a territory with borders and entry points in the human sense. Yet Jesus often speaks of the kingdom in spatial terms. When he does so he means that there is a kind of sacred space in which God's rule is exercised and recognised. This is why Jesus therefore uses spatial language when speaking of the kingdom.[23] It is something that can be entered and something that can be closed. 'How hard it will be for those who have riches to enter the kingdom of God' says Jesus at Mark 10.23. At Mark 10.15 Jesus says 'Truly I say to you, whoever does not receive the kingdom of God like a child shall never enter it'. In another passage the kingdom is described as a place to which people will come and sit at table to eat and drink. 'Men will come from east and west, and from north and south, and sit at table in the kingdom of God' says Jesus at Luke 13.29. Jesus promises to his disciples who have continued with him in his trials that 'I assign to you, as my Father assigned to me, a kingdom, that you may eat and drink at my table in my kingdom, and sit on thrones judging the twelve tribes of Israel' (Luke 22.29-30). After Peter has confessed at Caesarea Philippi that Jesus is the Christ, he is promised that to him will be given the keys of the kingdom of heaven (Matthew 16.19). At the Last Supper Jesus says, after distributing the cup, 'I shall not drink again of the fruit of the vine until that day when I drink it new in the kingdom of God' (Mark 14.25).

Now there is no doubt that the impression can easily be gained from some of these examples that Jesus is talking about something that is going to happen in the future; and that is certainly the case with the saying from Mark 14.25 about not drinking the fruit of the vine until the day that Jesus drinks it in the kingdom of God. He is looking beyond his death into what lies on the other side of it. There is undoubtedly a future dimension to the kingdom of God. It is therefore all the more

---

[23] See E. Lohmeyer, *Kultus und Evangelium*, Göttingen: Kommissionsverlag Vandenhoeck & Ruprecht, 1942, pp. 72-5.

important that we find ways of talking about the kingdom which express the fact that this dimension that belongs to the future is also very much a part of the present.

One way in which we may do this is as follows. In the Gospels, Jesus is portrayed as the creator of faith; as someone whose very presence helps people to have faith and trust that they did not have before. In the story of the woman with the incurable haemorrhage, she says to herself, 'if I touch even his garments, I shall be made well' (Mark 5.28). When she has done this, and Jesus identifies her as the one who touched him, he says to her, 'daughter, your faith has made you well; go in peace and be healed of you disease' (Mark 5.34). We can say that to the extent that Jesus was the creator of faith and trust, he was the kingdom of God coming to be present in the lives of those who were willing to be inspired by him. He was not simply a prophet promising to people that they would have a share in a future kingdom if their behaviour qualified them to do so. He was a part of that future kingdom that had come in the present to be where people were, enabling them by his very presence to be embraced by the kingdom. This is further borne out by the fact that in the ministry of Jesus the kingdom comes to embrace people who would not qualify for it on the basis of their behaviour.

One of the accusations made against Jesus by his opponents was that he welcomed tax collectors and sinners and ate with them (Luke 15.1). In Matthew 11.18, giving his opinion on John the Baptist, and how John's missions had been misunderstood, Jesus said 'John came neither eating or drinking, and they say, "He has a demon"; the Son of Man came eating and drinking, and they say, "Behold, a glutton and a drunkard, a friend of tax collectors and sinners!"'. The kingdom, then, is present in the person of Jesus and in that way touches the lives of people who have eyes to see it. His presence enables people to be embraced by the love and mercy of God.

There is an interesting implication of this. If the kingdom is a kind of sacred space entry into which is made possible by the faith that Jesus inspires, it is a rival to the Temple in Jerusalem. It was the Temple, after all, situated on Mount Zion, which was the place where God was to be sought, where sins were to be forgiven, where the various sacrifices were to be offered that marked the stages in human life and recalled the saving acts of God on behalf of his people. But if the presence of Jesus was a way into the presence of God, was there any longer any need for the Temple?

That the Temple could and would be destroyed was a theme of Old Testament prophecy. Micah, in the 8th century left his hearers in no doubt about this. 'Therefore because of you' (he was referring to the corrupt rulers, priests and prophets) 'Zion shall be ploughed as a field, Jerusalem shall become a heap of ruins, and the mountain of the house' (i.e. the Temple) 'a wooded height', (Micah 3.10). Jeremiah, similarly, reminded his hearers that God had destroyed the sanctuary of Shiloh where he had once caused his name to dwell, and that he would do the same to Jerusalem (Jeremiah 7.12-14). It is interesting that, at his trial, Jesus was accused of saying that he would destroy the Temple (Mark 14.38), and whether or not this was true, his ministry certainly had the practical effect of making the Temple irrelevant. If Jesus did destroy the Temple, this was not because he forecast its demise at the hand of an external foe (although the Gospel tradition did believe that he foresaw the destruction of the Temple by the Romans in AD 70; see, for example, Mark 13) it was because he made the Temple redundant by himself becoming the means by which people could come into the presence of God. We can say that God's sacred space, which the Temple embodied, had been transformed into the kingdom of God by the ministry of Jesus, and had come into the world in the ministry of Jesus.

The Kingdom as a dimension that confounds normal human logic

I have on several occasions in sermons in the Abbey drawn attention to features in the parables of Jesus that appear to be unfair or illogical. I think I have mentioned the occasion in my Durham days when I was talking about the parable of the Prodigal Son, and a woman who was present found the parable deeply offensive. She had put the care of her aged mother before her career and her marriage, and identified with the loyal son who had remained with his father, rather than with the irresponsible brother who had wasted his fortune and was now for some inexplicable reason given a royal welcome when he came crawling back to his father's house. I am sure we can all sympathise with how she felt.

In the parable of the Labourers in the Vineyard, where the workers who worked for six, three or even only one hour received the same pay as those who had worked for twelve hours, those who had worked for twelve hours were understandably aggrieved (Matthew 20.1-16). The most interesting example of the illogicality of the kingdom, for me, comes in that most misunderstood of parables, the parable of the Sheep and the Goats in Matthew 25.31-45. In the 1960s, especially, one heard too many sermons that told congregations that if they were generous in their giving to the poor and oppressed they were giving to Jesus, who was to be found in the poor and oppressed. Now I am not suggesting that it is a bad thing to give to the poor and oppressed, but this is not what the parable is about. The point of the parable comes when those who are admitted to the joy of their Lord have no idea why this should be so. 'Lord, when did we see thee hungry and feed thee, or thirsty and gave thee drink? And when did we see thee a stranger and welcome thee, or naked and clothe thee? And when did we see thee sick or in prison and visit thee'? Those who are told to depart to the fires prepared for the devil and his angels are equally adamant that they do not know why their fate has been thus decided, and they are convinced that they did all the right things. The brethren of Jesus, behaviour towards whom is the deciding factor, are not the poor and oppressed in general, but the disciples of Jesus, who are the nucleus of the kingdom.[24] The parable is about the hiddenness of the kingdom and the fact that people may support or deny it without knowing that they are doing this. It seems, on the face of it, totally unfair that the eternal fate of people should be decided by something of which they have no awareness.

Another example of the illogicality of the kingdom is seen in the parable of the Pearl of Great Price in Matthew 13.45. 'The kingdom of heaven is like a merchant in search of fine pearls, who, on finding one pearl of great value, went and sold all that he had and bought it'. From the practical point of view, what use to him was the pearl? Its purchase would leave him penniless. He could not eat it, and if he sold it in order to get the money to sustain his life, the whole point of him buying it in the first place would be lost!

These examples of unfairness and illogicality are not, of course, confined to the parables of Jesus. They also apply to his death on the cross. Even after two thousand years of getting used to the idea, it still seems absurd to point to an executed criminal and to say 'this is the Chosen Servant of God, whose death has brought salvation to the world.' For Paul, writing to Christians in Corinth only twenty years after the crucifixion it must have been even more illogical and

---

[24] The identity of the 'brothers' of the Son of Man is discussed by U. Luz, *Das Evangelium nach Matthäus (Evangelisch-Katholischer Kommentar zum Neuen Testament), Zürich: Benzinger Verlag; Neukirchen-Vluyn: Neukirchener Verlag, I/3, 1997, pp. 537-540.*

absurd. 'The word of the cross is folly to those who are perishing, but to us who are being saved it is the power of God...For Jews demand signs and Greeks seek wisdom, but we preach Christ crucified, a stumbling block to Jews and folly to Gentiles, but to those who are called, both Jews and Greeks, Christ the power of God and the wisdom of God. For the foolishness of God is wiser than men, and the weakness of God is stronger than men' (1 Corinthians 1.18, 22-25). The illogicality of the kingdom in the parables of Jesus is summed up in the absurdity of the cross.

The kingdom as something that resonates deeply with human emotions and aspirations

Some of the parables may seem illogical and absurd, but there are others that engage our emotions and tug at our heart strings. It was Oliver Quick who, in his book 'The Realism of Christ's Parables', drew attention to what he called 'Parables of Human Instinct'.[25] His two chief witnesses were the parables of the Lost Sheep and the Lost Coin in Luke 15.3-10. We all know what it is like to lose something. No matter how trivial it is, a pencil, or some keys or a sock, we have a feeling of frustration, a feeling of loss. And this feeling is out of all proportion to the fact that we have not lost 99.99 percent of our other belongings. We devote an amount of effort to finding the lost item which, again, is out of all proportion to its value in relation to all the things we have not lost; and when we find it, our joy at having done so is, again, out of all proportion to its importance in our lives. Our first impulse is to tell someone that we have found the lost item.

The parables of the Lost Sheep and the Lost Coin resonate with our common experience of losing and finding. No doubt the shepherd who has lost a sheep has an emotional

---

[25] O. C. Quick, *The Realism of Christ's Parables*. Ida Hartley Lectures delivered at Colne, Lancs, October 1930, London: SCM Press, 1931, pp. 29-39.

attachment to the animal that we would not have if we had lost a pen or a sock. Nevertheless, his feeling of loss and incompleteness leads him to behave in a somewhat reckless way in his pursuit of the animal. He leaves the ninety-nine other sheep and goes off to look for the lost one. Who will look after the ninety-nine in his absence? Might they become a target for wild animals or thieves? No doubt he is fully aware of these risks, but is prepared to take them, so overwhelming is his desire to get back the lost sheep. It comes as no surprise to read that when he finds it, he calls his friends and his neighbours together to share with him in his joy and relief.

In the case of the woman who has lost the coin, we do not know whether it is valuable, perhaps part of a precious necklace that is her insurance policy if her husband divorces her, or whether it is simply some sort of simple ornament. Whatever it is, she searches diligently for the lost item, and again, asks her friends and neighbours to share in her joy when she finds it. But these two parables are not simply stories about the human experience of losing and finding. They are parables of the kingdom of God, and they end with the words 'there will be more joy in heaven over one sinner who repents than over ninety-nine righteous persons who need no repentance'. Our human feelings of joy at finding something lost are replicated in the presence of God. Moreover, the recklessness with which we search for what is lost is replicated by God's recklessness in coming into our world in Jesus Christ, defenceless and hidden, to seek to win out allegiance. If we want to know what God thinks of us and to what lengths he is prepared to go to find us, then the parables of the Lost Sheep and Lost Coin in particular give us the answer, by appealing to our own emotions; and this is an important clue as to how we can begin to see the kingdom of God and find ourselves embraced by it.

In my sermon at the Abbey last Sunday, based on the incident in which Jesus is accused of casting out demons by being in league with Satan, I pointed out that although Jesus clearly won the argument with his opponents at the level of logic, the matter could not be left there because the kingdom of God is not something to be proved by logical argument. It does not belong to that level of reality. Instead, I mentioned the importance of the incident at the end of Luke's Gospel in which the Risen Lord walks from Jerusalem to Emmaus on the first Easter Day with two disciples (Luke 24.-33). You will remember the story. As they walk, the two disciples are discussing the tragedy of the death of Jesus and how this has dashed all the hopes that they had had in him. A stranger, who is the risen Lord, meets them and accompanies them on their journey. It is significant that he hides his true identity from them. He does not try to force them into the kingdom by a display of power. He does not say, 'I am Jesus, who was dead and is now alive'. As he walks with them, he simply tries to explain things. His aim is to help them make sense of what has happened, and he does this by explaining the scriptures and how they refer to the necessity of God's chosen Servant having to suffer and then enter into his glory. His aim is not to convince them from above, so to speak, but to enable them to be certain from within, as things begin to make sense to them. This is the way of the kingdom.

The fact that many parables seem to be illogical and unfair does not mean that, ultimately, we are being asked to believe in nonsense. The scandal of the death of Jesus as God's way of salvation, and the unfairness of some of the parables can, in fact, make sense, especially when they are seen as part of the unfathomable love and mercy of God, the exercise of which in the world of human greed, anger and compensation culture is bound to be seen as illogical. The parables of the Lost Sheep and Lost Coin can put us, through our own feelings, in touch with that unfathomable love of God and help us to begin to make sense of something that is so much greater than our own world that it can only be spoken of in parables whose view of the world seems strange and sometimes unfair.

But this world is also a world of generosity. The Prodigal Son is given a new start in life, the workers in the vineyard who had been unemployed all day are given a full wage with which to feed and support their families, the Good Samaritan pays at the inn for the upkeep and recuperation of the robbed man, whom he has never met before. If only we could live in such a world, a world in which the first instincts in human behaviour were always driven by love and generosity! It is also possible for our hope for this kind of world, a kingdom of right relationships, to resonate with what I was describing in the first lecture as the heart-hunger that comes from our mysterious encounters with the sacred and the numinous. Might it be that those feelings that are so difficult to describe and which are yet so real, can make sense in the light of the kingdom of God as preached by Jesus? If we wish to translate those heart-hungers into a committed way of life, might not the answer be that we can do so by becoming followers of Jesus and disciples of the kingdom?

There is one last matter to be mentioned before I conclude, and it goes back to John the Baptist's expectation that the coming day of the Lord would be a time of the judgement of evil. Is the coming of the kingdom in the ministry of Jesus a judgement of evil? Some of the parables do, of course, mention judgement after death, for example, the parable of the Rich Man and Lazarus in Luke 16.19-31. But there are more ways of judging evil than zapping it with force, or defeating it with its own weapons. Evil is judged by the cross. The crucifixion shows up evil in its true colours in many ways, yet evil is unable to defeat the one who prays incessantly 'Father forgive them'. The coming of the kingdom in Jesus does involve the judgement of evil and all that is wrong in human nature, but just as the kingdom is hidden, so evil is defeated in a way that does not conform to human standards of dealing with wrong. The cross, we can say, is part of the mystery of the kingdom.

In Luke 17.20 Jesus as asked when the kingdom of God is coming. He replies, 'The kingdom of God is not coming with signs to be observed; nor will they say, "Lo, here it is!" or "There!" for behold, the kingdom of God is within you'. This well-known saying is in fact a mistranslation of the Greek *entos humôn*, which means 'among you' or 'in your midst'. That saying is as true for us as it was for the first hearers of Jesus. It has been said that the kingdom of God came into our world not only in the ministry of Jesus but also in his words.[26] Those words are available to us today in the Gospels and, indeed, we have been considering them in this lecture. They can enable us to be grasped by the mystery of the kingdom, to glimpse it, to enter into it, to call us to become disciples of the kingdom by being disciples of Jesus. The kingdom of God is in our midst!

The two most profound interpreters of Jesus in the New Testament were St. Paul and the writer of St. John's Gospel. How did they understand and interpret Jesus's message of the kingdom of God? That is the subject of next week's lecture.

---

[26] See E. Lohmeyer, 'Vom Sinn der Gleichnisse Jesu' in Lohmeyer, *Urchristliche Mystik. Neutestamentliche Studien*, Darmstadt: Wissenschaftliche Buchgesellschaft, 1958, pp. 125-157.

LECTURE 4

The Kingdom of God in Paul and John

There is a remarkable statistic in the New Testament. The Greek word *basileia*, meaning 'kingdom', occurs 111 times in the Gospels of Matthew, Mark and Luke, although not all of them, of course, are used as part of the phrase 'kingdom of God'. In the remainder of the New Testament *basileia* occurs only fifty-one times.[27] This is usually explained by saying that the notion of the kingdom of God was a Jewish idea that did not resonate easily in the Graeco-Roman world into which early Christianity spread, so that other ways were found of expressing the same idea. In the main letters of Paul the phrase 'kingdom of God' occurs only four times and in John's Gospel it occurs only twice. However, two of these occurrences in Paul and John are important and will be

---

[27] R. Morgenthaler, *Statistik des neutestamentlichen Wortschatzes*, Zürich: Gotthelf-Verlag, 1958, p. 82.

discussed later in the lecture. They are Romans 14.17: 'the kingdom of God is not food and drink (Paul is discussing food regulations) but righteousness and peace and joy in the Holy Spirit' and John 3.3, 'truly I say to you, unless one is born anew, he cannot see the kingdom of God'. However, the absence of the phrase 'kingdom of God' does not mean the absence of the idea, and the aim of this lecture is to show how what was said last week about the kingdom of God in the teaching of Jesus, is worked out in Paul and John. I begin with the teaching of Jesus on the kingdom as a kind of sacred space.

I said last week that for Jesus the kingdom of God is a kind of sacred space in which God's rule is exercised, and which, in the person of Jesus comes to be a factor in the lives of people that enables them to draw close to God. I said that this had the effect of making the Temple in Jerusalem redundant as the place where the presence of God was to be sought, and I pointed out that prophets such as Micah and Jeremiah had foretold the destruction of the Temple by God himself, and that Jesus was accused at his trial of saying that he would destroy the Temple.

The Temple in Jerusalem in the time of Jesus and Paul consisted of a great courtyard, divided into several zones. Non-Jews were forbidden to enter any part of the sacred courtyard. The first zone within the courtyard was the court of women, there then followed the court of men who were not priests or levites, and finally there was the area permitted only to priests and levites. For Paul, what God had done in Jesus Christ had abolished the barriers that separated non-Jews from Jews and men from women and, he added, slaves from those who were free. 'There is neither Jew nor Greek, there is neither slave nor free, there is neither male nor female; for you are all one in Christ Jesus' Paul proclaimed in Galatians 3.28. Jesus had, in effect, abolished the Temple by abolishing the barriers that separated Jews from non-Jews and men from women in the presence of God. We can say that for Paul, what he calls 'Christ Jesus' has become the sacred space in which God's kingdom is present and his rule is exercised. By 'Christ Jesus' Paul means a sacred space made possible by the ministry, death and exaltation of Jesus, a space into which people can enter by the grace of God, and in which they experience the presence of the God and Father of Jesus Christ in company with other members of the kingdom. This idea of Jesus as the sacred space of the kingdom is fully in accord with what we find in Jesus's own ministry, where his presence draws into the presence of God the tax collectors and sinners, among others. The idea of Christ as sacred space is further developed by Paul in 1 Corinthians 15 and Romans 5, where Adam and Christ are contrasted as two types of humanity, one belonging to the present, transient or passing world, the other, representing God's eternal kingdom which is entered here and now. 'As in Adam all die, so in Christ shall all be made alive' is the triumphant claim of Paul in 1 Corinthians 15.22.

One of the features of John's Gospel is that the signs that Jesus performs are used by the writer of the Gospel to introduce teaching of Jesus about who he is and what his mission is. The cleansing of the Temple, in which Jesus casts out the money changers from the Temple occurs at the beginning of John's Gospel, unlike the other Gospels where the incident is placed at the beginning of Holy Week, and in John it introduces the whole topic of Jesus and the destruction of the Temple. Jesus is asked by his opponents what sign he can give to justify what he has done in casting out the money changers and traders. He replies, 'Destroy this temple, and in three days I will raise it up' (John 2.19). The opponents reply that it has taken forty-six years to build it – they are probably referring to the rebuilding undertaken by Herod the Great – and how can Jesus raise it up in three days? The writer of the Gospel comments that Jesus was speaking of the temple of his body and, by implication his resurrection; but John's Gospel is a text that must always be read between the lines, and the German commentator Ernst Haenchen is surely correct to comment that the writer has in view the destruction of the Temple cult, and that the narrative is looking forward to the dialogue between Jesus and the Samaritan woman in chapter 4 in which Jesus says that the 'true worshippers of God do not believe that God is close to people on Mount Zion or Mount Gerizim but that God is always present to believers in Jesus and the words of Jesus'.[28] This is fully in accordance with Jesus's own proclamation of the kingdom as a sacred space that has come into the world in his person and which brings people into the presence of God.

Something that I did not discuss last week but which must be considered now is the relationship between the kingdom of God and the law, by which I mean the law graciously revealed to his people by God after he had released them from slavery in Egypt. This is a complicated subject, which I shall have to over-simplify, and content myself with saying that for many devout Jews in the time of Jesus and Paul, observance of the law was a not a way of gaining God's favour, but a way of showing gratitude to God for his love and mercy. It followed from this, however, that those who broke the law or who were indifferent to it were indifferent to God's love and promises to his people. In the ministry of Jesus, his apparent breaking of the law and his association with 'sinners' could be interpreted by opponents as his own indifference to God's love and mercy, things that made it impossible for him to be the chosen Servant of God. In fact, in the ministry of Jesus the coming of the kingdom of God does not abolish the law, but puts it into a new perspective. The kingdom of God is the exercise of God's freedom to be God in his own way and not according to human expectations, and it is this that leads Jesus into conflict

---

[28] E. Haenchen, 'Johanneische Probleme' in *Zeitschrift für Theologie und Kirche*, 56 (1959), p. 46, my translation.

with his opponents. Jesus heals people on the Sabbath day, and the argument that he should heal on a different day out of respect for the Sabbath is a reasonable argument. But the kingdom of God is an expression of the reaching out of divine love to wherever there is human need, so that the priority becomes the freeing of humans from what diminishes their wholeness. 'The Sabbath is made for man, not man for the Sabbath'. The kingdom of God does not abolish the law, but puts it into a new context.

The status of the divine law is an important issue for both Paul and the writer of John's Gospel. At the personal level, and this may have been bound up with Paul's particular character, the observance of the divine law had become enslaving rather than liberating, and Paul's discovery that God's love towards him had been expressed in the Son of God 'who loved me and gave himself for me' to quote Galatians 2.20, totally transformed his relation to the law. We might say that just as Jesus in his earthly ministry changed the lives of people by entering into friendship with them in a process that by-passed the law, so to speak, Paul's discovery that the Son of God had loved him and given himself for him also meant a coming to know God that was independent of the divine law. Paul therefore saw that while the law was 'holy, just and good', to quote Romans 7.12, it could also be a barrier to coming to know God. That was at the personal level, but there was another dimension also.

I have already said this evening that for Paul, Christ was the sacred space of the kingdom that abolished distinctions between Jews and non-Jews and between men and women. The divine law as it had come to be elaborated in later Judaism also created barriers between Jews and non-Jews and between men and women, and if the coming of the kingdom of God in Jesus had abolished those barriers in respect of the Temple, then it had also abolished them in regard to the law.

This was at the heart of the bitter dispute in the early church between the so-called Judaising Christians, who believed that non-Jews who became Christians should be circumcised and observe the law of Moses, and Paul and his supporters who believed that this compromised what God had done for the whole human race in Jesus. How serious this could become at the practical level is shown by the fact that, as Paul tells us in Galatians, when Peter (called Cephas in Galatians 2.11-14) came to Antioch he was initially prepared to eat with Gentile believers, but refused to do so when representatives of the Judaising Christian party arrived.

In John's Gospel the matter of the law is approached differently, but consistently with the implications of the coming of the kingdom of God in the ministry of Jesus. As usual in this Gospel it is a sign that Jesus performs that is the occasion of a dialogue between Jesus and his opponents. We can take as representative, John chapter 5, the healing of the lame man at the Pool of Bethesda. The miracle is related without any hint that it has been performed on the Sabbath. Once the lame man is healed he is told by Jesus to take up his pallet and walk. It is only then that we are told that it is the Sabbath and that the healed man is accused by the religious authorities that it is unlawful to carry a pallet on the Sabbath. The healed man is ignorant of who it is that has healed him and told him to carry the pallet, but after he has discovered that it is Jesus, and he has told the authorities, a bitter dispute takes place between Jesus and the authorities. The chapter is far too long to be summarised here, but at issue is the authority of Jesus as the Son of God. We have to remember that John's Gospel is not telling us what was actually said during the ministry of Jesus, but is constructing a narrative to bring out the full implications of the meaning of the earthly ministry of Jesus. John's Gospel is claiming that Jesus's breaking of the law occurs because he is greater than the law, because he is the unique Son of God. This claim does full justice to what happens in the earthly ministry of Jesus in which the presence in him of the kingdom of God makes the law take a second place to the active love of God which is at the heart of the kingdom.

In the second part of this lecture I want to discuss how it is that Paul and John deal with the fact that in the ministry of Jesus the kingdom of God, which is a future phenomenon, has already arrived in the world and is active in it. The key terms are, for Paul, the righteousness of God (*dikaiosunē theou*)[29] and the Holy Spirit, and for John the concept of eternal life.

'I am not ashamed of the gospel' writes Paul in Romans 1.16, 'it is the power of God for salvation to every one who has faith, to the Jew first and also to the Greek. For in it the righteousness of God is revealed through faith for faith'. The phrase 'righteousness of God' resonates deeply with passages such as Psalm 103.6, 'the LORD works righteousness and justice for all who are oppressed with wrong'. Although this verse is not a declaration of the effects of the coming Day of the Lord, it draws upon that bundle of ideas. God works to bring judgement against what is wrong, and vindication (which is what the Hebrew word for righteousness means in the psalm) for all who are oppressed. He engages actively on behalf of the wronged and the oppressed. For Paul, God's righteousness similarly means God's engagement on behalf of a human race oppressed by structural and individual wrongness, a condition that Paul sums up in the word 'sin'. God's righteousness works by assuring people that God justifies the ungodly through faith in the Crucified and Risen Christ, a faith that God himself makes possible and inspires. However, this complicated theological formulation does not differ essentially from the simple picture in the Gospels, of

---

[29] See E. Jüngel, *Paulus und Jesus. Eine Untersuchung zur Präzisierung der Frage nach dem Urpsrung der Christologie*, Tübingen: Mohr Siebeck, 7th ed., 2004, p. 266.

Jesus offering his friendship to people including the sinners and the outcast, and by this friendship transforming their lives, giving them faith and hope they would not otherwise be capable of having. The difference between Jesus and Paul is that in the ministry of Jesus it is the physical presence of Jesus that is the transforming factor, while for Paul it is the preaching of the Cross that is the transformative factor.

In both cases, that is, of Jesus and Paul, something decisive has happened to change not just individuals, but the world in which they live. In Jesus the kingdom of God is present. For Paul, the death of Jesus has destroyed the evil age which dominates peoples' lives; as he writes at the beginning of Galatians, Jesus Christ 'gave himself for our sins to deliver us from the present evil age according to the will of our God and Father' (Galatians 1.4). We can say that for Paul, the idea of the 'righteousness of God' actively defeating evil and bringing people into a new relationship with God is the equivalent of the coming of the kingdom of God in the ministry of Jesus. However, Paul also uses another idea to express most strongly his conviction that the age to come has dawned, and that is his appeal to the presence of the Holy Spirit.

One of the puzzles of the New Testament is the fact that whereas Paul has much to say about the Holy Spirit, the expression is hardly used at all by Jesus. This is something that I discussed in my book 'The Holy Spirit in Biblical and Pastoral Perspective', basing myself very much upon the brilliant book 'The Holy Spirit and the Gospel Tradition' by my former colleague and good friend in Durham, the late Kingsley Barrett.[30] I shall not repeat the argument here. However, as I pointed out in the second lecture, the gift of the

[30] J. W. Rogerson, *The Holy Spirit in Biblical and Pastoral Perspective*, Sheffield: Beauchief Abbey Press, 2013; C. K. Barrett, *The Holy Spirit and the Gospel Tradition*, London: SPCK, 1966.

Holy Spirit was very much associated in the Old Testament with the coming of the Day of the Lord in the prophetic traditions, and especially that in the book of Joel. For Paul, the presence of the Holy Spirit in the church is an indication that an important feature of the age to come has indeed come into the world, and he goes so far as to call the gift of the Holy Spirit a 'first instalment' or *arrabon* to quote the Greek (2 Corinthians 1.22, 5.5). It is worth spending a moment to think through the implications of this.

A first instalment is something concrete and tangible. When I get an advance of royalties for a book (not usually very much for I am far from being in the J. K. Rowling league) it is because an agreement has been signed and a book has been written and published. I have money in hand which I can spend and I have the guarantee that more will come in the future, unless the publisher ceases to trade, something which has, unfortunately, happened to me twice! The first instalment, of which Paul speaks, is therefore a promise connected with the future but which is a present and tangible fact. It is not a vague promise about something that is to come in another world. It is a real factor in this world but also something that guarantees what is to come in the future.

I have been talking about 'it', but of course Paul is speaking about the Holy Spirit, and it is no accident that the supreme description of the Holy Spirit is in terms of love, *agape*, in 1 Corinthians 13. Kingsley Barrett commented on this chapter that while the definition of love in it tended to shift in meaning, 'it becomes apparent not only that the only human model he can have used is Jesus of Nazareth, but that the description is a description of the love of God, who alone loves spontaneously and without motivation'.[31] In Jesus,

---

[31] C. K. Barrett, *The First Epistle to the Corinthians* (Black's New Testament Commentaries), London: A. & C. Black, 1968, p. 310.

God's love becomes incarnate. For Paul, that 'incarnation' is found in the Holy Spirit; and divine love is at the heart of the kingdom of God.

This brings me to the text that I referred to earlier, from Romans 14.17, 'the kingdom of God is not food and drink but righteousness and peace and joy in the Holy Spirit'. This verse brings together the two key terms that I have been discussing, the righteousness of God and the Holy Spirit. While Paul probably means by righteousness in this verse a life lived righteously, for him this is made possible only by the righteousness of God which creates a new relationship, in which the Holy Spirit makes possible peace and joy as well as righteousness.

In John's Gospel, it is the concept of eternal life that enables the writer to say that something belonging to the future has become a part of the present. It is also interesting that the phrases 'kingdom of God' and 'eternal life' occur close to each other in chapter 3 of the Gospel. In his commentary on John, Kingsley Barrett comments as follows at that point,

> It is clear from consideration of the passages enumerated above, in which eternal life is mentioned, that the concept retains something of its original eschatological [i.e. futuristic] connection, but also that it may equally be thought of as a present gift of God; in this, *zoē aiônios* in John resembles 'kingdom of God' in the synoptic gospels. That which is properly a future blessing becomes a present fact in virtue of the realization of the future in Christ.[32]

In this connection it is unfortunate that William Tyndale translated the Greek *zoē aiônios* as 'everlasting life', something that was followed by the King James version and which found

---

[32] C. K. Barrett, *The Gospel According to St. John. An Introduction with Commentary and Notes on the Greek Text*, London: SPCK, 1958, p. 179.

its way into the Book of Common Prayer. Whatever it may have conveyed to readers in the 16th and 17th centuries, the phrase 'everlasting' in our times has tended to place the emphasis on the quantity rather than the quality of the life being spoken of. In fact, the Greek zoē aiōnios is not referring to something that begins after death and which goes on for ever and ever; it is referring to something that is available now, in this life, and which is characterised by a quality which marks it off from what is normally understood as 'life'. In John's Gospel it is bound up indissolubly with fellowship with Jesus. It is not, as the impression can easily be given in church or at funerals, a kind of immortality, a living for ever, unconnected with God; it is precisely because it is friendship with Jesus, to use a phrase that I have used earlier in the lecture, that it is life of a particular quality. We are all familiar with the way in which friendships and being with particular people can profoundly affect life as we live it. In the case of the eternal life spoken of in John's Gospel, it is the life of God realised in the offer of the friendship of Jesus. Many passages in the Gospel make this clear.

> God so loved the world that he gave his only Son, that whoever believes in him should not perish but have eternal life (John 3.16).

> He who believes in the Son has eternal life (John 3.36).

> My sheep hear my voice, and I know them, and they follow me; and I give them eternal life, and they shall never perish, and no one shall snatch them out of my hand (John 10.27-8).

It is important to recognise that 'to believe in' Jesus in this context does not primarily mean to believe things about him, for example, that he is the Son of God. Just as in the case of earthly friends we are prepared to trust them and to commit ourselves to them to a greater or lesser degree, so to 'believe in' Jesus means to trust that his paradoxical way of weakness and hiddenness, his vision of a world whose values often seem to contradict what we may think makes for sense and justice, in fact represents the will of God; that it discloses to us a God who may be unlike how we think he ought to be. We can say that eternal life as spoken of in John's Gospel is the equivalent of having entered the kingdom of God as it is brought near and expressed in the words of Jesus, in the first three Gospels.

The most interesting passage connected with the kingdom of God in John's Gospel is, as I have already mentioned, to be found in the third chapter. A Pharisee and a ruler of the Jews named Nicodemus comes to Jesus by night to try to find out who Jesus is. Unlike the opponents of Jesus in the incident in Matthew 12 who draw the conclusion that the signs that are performed by Jesus indicate that he is in league with the devil, Nicodemus concedes that Jesus must be a teacher sent from God, otherwise he would not be able to perform such signs. Jesus does not allow the conversation to remain at the level of logical argument, even though it is being conducted in a friendly way. He replies to Nicodemus that unless one is born anew he cannot see the kingdom of God. There is a long and profound observation on this in Barrett's commentary which deserves to be partly quoted.

> [Born anew] may mean 'from above', but also 'afresh', 'again'. The birth that is here required is certainly a second birth, but it is not...a mere repetition of man's first birth, but a begetting from above, from God...The novelty of John's thought when compared with Judaism is not accidental, since the point of this paragraph is to bring out the fact that the Old Testament religion and Judaism, which Nicodemus the Pharisee and ruler of the Jews, the teacher of Israel, represents, is inadequate; it cannot move forward continuously into the kingdom of God. A moment of discontinuity, comparable with physical birth, is essential. Man as such, even the Israelite, is not by nature capable of the kingdom of God...The

source of the new terminology is primarily the primitive gospel tradition...Together with these sayings about entering and receiving the kingdom of God must be taken...the fundamental New Testament assertion about the kingdom of God, namely, that not merely is it to be expected in its fullness in the age to come, but it has already been manifested, germinally or potentially, in the person and work of Jesus.[33]

John's Gospel does not contain any of the parables of the kingdom of God as we find them in Matthew, Mark and Luke, but it certainly implies them in this passage. The kingdom is not a matter of logic or a demonstration of supernatural power; it is about seeing things in a new and different way, a seeing that is allied to what happens when something that has puzzled us suddenly makes sense and we experience a feeling of intellectual exhilaration, and our whole way of understanding what is going on around us is from that point different.

I have tried to show in this lecture that although the phrase 'kingdom of God' occurs rarely in Paul and in John's Gospel it is present by being interpreted in new ways. How can, or should, today's church interpret and present the kingdom in its mission to the world? That is the subject of the last lecture, next Wednesday.

---

[33] Barrett, *John*, pp. 171-2.

LECTURE 5

The Kingdom of God
and the Church Today

I must begin with a confession. The lectures that you have been hearing this Lent have been partly autobiographical, and because that will affect what I say today about the kingdom of God and the church, it is important that you know where I am coming from and why. The first lecture began with the kingdom of heaven as explored by Arthur Clutton-Brock. It discussed those experiences of the holy and the numinous which produced, in the memorable phrase of John Ruskin, a kind of heart hunger. This is where my own path into Christian faith began.

Neither of my parents' families had had any connection with organised Christianity for generations, as far as I know, and so my first exposure to organised religion was through the Christian hymns, prayers, and readings from the Bible at the daily assembly at secondary school. These, however, did not affect me particularly in any way. What affected me, were the walks that I did as a teenager on the South Downs near Guildford and Reigate in Surrey, together with the English folk song inspired music of Ralph Vaughan Williams and Gustav Holst. These certainly inspired feelings that can be described as heart hunger, and which meant that the obsession of my life in my teenage years was music. A significant point in my life in which the kingdom of heaven became the kingdom of God was attendance at evensong in 1954 on the first Sunday after Trinity. I was on leave from my National Service in the Royal Air Force and went to my local church, Saint Andrew's, Earlsfield, in South London. It had been built at the end of the 19th century and had an imposing high altar and sanctuary. Although it was situated on a main road, there was little traffic on a Sunday evening in 1954, and the church had a marvellous atmosphere of stillness and coolness compared with the warmth outside. The simple liturgical service, the prayers which had a worldwide concern, and the sermon which was based on the gospel for the day, the Parable of the Rich Man and Lazarus, all enabled me to connect the heart-hunger feelings of the kingdom of heaven with the kingdom of God as expressed in Christian worship and witness. That experience was neither the beginning nor the end of my journey into faith but it was an important milestone. It set me on to an intensive study of the parables of Jesus and of his teaching on the kingdom of God, and determined my future as one who wished to become a fulltime disciple of Jesus, in the ordained ministry.

I still had one important step to take. In churches that I attended there was little or no attention paid to the parables of Jesus or his teaching about the kingdom of God. I heard a great deal about 'The Lord Jesus Christ' about whom I was expected to believe certain things, especially how God had punished him so that the sins of mankind could be forgiven.

What I had to do was to connect what I found in the writings of Paul and the Gospel of John with what I found in the first three gospels, and indeed, this was what the fourth of this year's lectures was concerned with. I shall come back to this later, but it exemplified the theological problem of how Jesus who is the witness to faith and the author of faith in the first three gospels becomes the object of faith in the writings of Paul, John's Gospel, and the creeds and formularies of the church. We are back to Clutton-Brock's inquirer in the first lecture who looked in vain in the creeds and formularies for information about the kingdom of God. I shall not say anything more about my own path into faith, but hope that what I have said will become clearer as the lecture proceeds.

The fact that it was a church service which for me made the connection between the kingdom of heaven and the kingdom of God has always made me concerned that whatever else worship did, it should convey something of the mystery and majesty of God; that it should be something that not merely engaged the mind and thought, but something that engaged the emotions. This means that, aesthetically, I have never found it easy to engage in the kind of non-liturgical worship that used to characterise the free churches in our country and which seem increasingly to be a feature of some of the Anglican churches. Ideally, Christian worship should convey something of the numinous, and although I am not particularly high church myself, it is in high church services that I have found that element to be more frequently present.

Here at the Abbey, I am grateful for the very small fact that the geography of the present chapel means that celebrants at the service of Holy Communion must stand with their backs to the congregation. There is, of course, the rather charming story in Gregory Dix's book 'The Shape of the Liturgy', a book written when celebrants always had their backs to their congregations. He recalls what I think one of his aunts had been told. This was that at a particular point in the communion service, a live crab was released on the altar and it was the job of the officiating priest to make sure that no one in the congregation saw it, and that the gestures and motions through which the celebrant went came about because he was trying to catch the unfortunate creature without the congregation seeing it! I must confess that when I go to communion services where celebrants face the congregation I sometimes become too aware of the manual actions which are being performed during the service. Perhaps I should not be looking, but I often find them off putting and not conducive to getting some sense of the numinous at that point in the service. No one obviously wishes to see celebrants with their backs to the congregation behaving as though they were trying to conceal a crab, but I wonder if celebrants who face congregations realise how off putting their visible actions can be to the congregations they face?

Another factor here concerns the liturgy that is used. The Anglican Church has become very wordy. Congregations are faced either with books containing various liturgies, or words are projected on to screens. There is something to be said for having the same liturgy each week which people know by heart and which can enable them to concentrate their minds on the significance of what is happening rather than concentrating upon reading the words presented to them. The use of Elizabethan English may also enable the liturgy to convey a certain dignity and detachment from the present world. Although I would not want to advocate having services in Latin, I can quite understand that the use of the Latin to which congregations had become accustomed, could have played an enormous part in conveying the sense of the holy and the numinous in worship. This may all sound very reactionary and there may well be much better ways of meeting the points that I am trying to make. However, I think that it is a serious issue that the church today has to face, and it is interesting that the Nine O'Clock service which was aimed at the sort of young person familiar with the club scene in Sheffield used, in addition to contemporary music, ancient liturgies including Latin, so that there would be in the worship an element of the holy and the numinous.

Let me pass from the form of worship to the content of the church's preaching. Here we meet the problem of the distinction between Jesus as the witness to faith and the inspirer of faith, and Jesus as the object of faith.[34] Should the emphasis of the church's preaching be upon Jesus as the witness to faith and the inspirer of faith, or on Jesus as the object of faith? On the face of it, there is surely nothing to be discussed. 'Jesus Christ is the same yesterday and today and for ever' we are reminded in the letter to the Hebrews (Hebrews 13.8). If, during his earthly ministry, Jesus inspired people to have faith in God, then surely he can do the same today, and the church's task is to acquaint people with his teaching, especially his parables. After all, are we able to improve upon the parable of the Good Samaritan, or of the Labourers in the Vineyard, or the parables of the Great Feast, or of the Lost Sheep and the Lost Coin? Surely, all that we have to do is to acquaint people with the teaching of Jesus and rely in faith and trust upon his power to create faith in them. This might seem to be the obvious answer, and yet time and again the church and its methods of evangelism have taken the other course. I can remember being at missions to more than one university where, having tried to prove the existence of God, the missioner has then tried to prove the divinity of Jesus. One sometimes comes across the argument that is found in C.S. Lewis. Jesus claimed to be the Son of God. Either he was a liar, or he was mad, or he was speaking the truth, with the implication that we must accept the latter, that he was

---

[34] See the discussion in G. Ebeling, *The Nature of Faith*, London: Collins, 1966, chapters iv and v.

speaking the truth and therefore must believe that he was the Son of God. However, this is believing **that** not believing **in**. Surely this is the wrong approach.

Given that within our services we expect people to recite the creeds, creeds that are concerned with Jesus as the object of faith rather than as the witness to and inspirer of faith, it seems to me that we must go out of our way to put as much emphasis as possible on Jesus as the one who is the inspirer of faith. This is where the preaching should be concentrated, and the Christian faith should be presented as discipleship, as following Jesus today. But it will also be necessary, in study groups, so to study the writings of Paul and the Gospel of John that these, too, are then understood to bear witness to Jesus as the creator of faith rather than faith's object. There are several wise sayings that point our thoughts in that direction. For example, it has been said that it is not the cross that saves, but Christ, but the Christ of the cross. Or, to take another example, to believe in the resurrection is not to believe that Jesus rose from the dead, but to believe in the risen Christ. Sermons that try to prove that the only possible answer to the question 'what happened on Easter day?' is that Christ must have risen from the dead confuse the issue between believing in Christ and believing about Christ. If we can get this right, this will be an important gain in our evangelistic outreach. It will also tackle the next topic about which we must think. If we preach Jesus as the witness to faith and as the inspirer of faith, we shall have to concentrate also on what he said about the kingdom of God. If the emphasis is on Jesus as the object of faith, little will be said about the kingdom of God, and we shall find ourselves in the situation of Clutton-Brock's inquirer who could find nothing about the kingdom of heaven in the creeds and formularies of the church.

But there is another consequence of concentrating upon Jesus as the object of faith, and that is the loss of the sense of urgency in the mission and preaching of Jesus. Jesus proclaimed that the kingdom of God was at hand, and as I explained in the first lecture, we can think of this in the sense of a taxi having arrived to take us to some destination. The taxi is not about to come, or just around the corner; it is present, and its presence is affecting my situation here and now. Jesus's proclamation that the kingdom of God is at hand is that something has happened, and that that event is now radically affecting the present. To concentrate upon Jesus as the object of faith and to ignore his actual teaching is to risk missing out on this vital element in his message.

As it so often happens in the history of the church, things that are neglected in mainstream churches find ways of being emphasised at what we might call the margins of the church. Thus, for example, there are churches which pay a great deal of attention to the Second Coming of Jesus, even sometimes to the point of believing that it is to happen so soon that members are discouraged from taking out Life Insurance on the ground that they will not need it because the world will soon come to an end. As I shall argue shortly, this kind of belief in the Second Coming misunderstands what Jesus meant by the 'end'.

Another interesting form that concern about Jesus and the future takes, is in what is called in American fundamentalism pre-millenarianism and post-millenarianism.[35] There are theological institutions in the United States that take these things so seriously, that students studying there have to subscribe their belief in pre-millenarianism or post-millenarianism as the case may be. These beliefs are based upon 1 Corinthians 15.24-6 and Revelation 20.4, and take two

---

[35] See G. M. Marsden, *Fundamentalism and American Culture. The Shaping of Twentieth Century Evangelicalism 1870-1925*, New York: Oxford University Press 1980,

forms. One form, pre-millenarianism, is the belief that the present age is the age dominated by Satan, and that the Second Coming of Christ will put an end to this dominion, and inaugurate the rule of 1000 years which is described in Revelation 20.4. The other view is that the death and resurrection of Jesus have inaugurated the new millennium, that Christ now rules within it, and that the end will come when Christ hands over everything to the father, as in 1 Corinthians 15.24-6. One interesting consequence of pre-millenarianism, which is probably the predominant view among American fundamentalists, is that it is wrong to engage in the environmental movement to save the planet from global warming. If the present age is dominated by Satan, then global warming and natural catastrophes are signs that Satan's dominion is beginning to weaken. Therefore, any attempt to prevent global warming and its consequences is in effect assisting Satan to maintain his hold over the present age. This view encourages certain groups to deny that there is evidence for global warming and to deny that anything should be done to mitigate its effects. This is a terribly serious consequence of what happens when the message of Jesus about the end is misunderstood.

In order to try to understand the teaching of Jesus about the end, it is necessary to define two senses of end. The best way I can do this, and there may be better ways, is by thinking of an extremely well written detective novel. It may be 379 pages long. If you are reading page 200, you can say that the end will come at page 379. However, there is another sense in which the novel has an end, and that is the point at which much that has been obscure during the course of the novel will become clear. The guilty person will be unmasked, and clues that pointed towards him or her earlier in the novel will now make sense. The end, therefore, will not just simply mean the last page, but the conclusion which makes sense of everything which has gone before.

Imagine now that you are reading that novel for the second time, or that you have cheated by looking at the last pages before you finished reading it. If you now already know how the novel concludes, you will read it in a quite different way compared with reading it when you do not know how it will end. You will see where the clues are pointing to, whereas previously you did not necessarily know that they were clues, or what they amounted to. This may not be a very good illustration of what I'm trying to say, but when Jesus says that the kingdom of God has arrived, he means that the end that will make sense of everything is already present, operating in the world, and making sense of what may not seem to be particularly logical. It is here I think that we must locate those elements in the parables that seem to us to be illogical and unfair. In the parable of the Prodigal Son, for example, a value (that of overwhelming and undeserved grace) is being revealed which is part of the end that is now present in the world, but which seems so contradictory to our notions of fairness and loyalty, although deeper study of the parable may help us to appreciate that value and why it is so important that it should play a part in our world. My criticism of those who concentrate upon the Second Coming or on pre-millenarianism is that they have misunderstood what Jesus meant by the end. They are thinking of the last pages of the novel as opposed to that end of the novel which makes sense of what is going on in the course of its pages.

Another way of putting this is that Christians should have a lively sense that they are living in two ages, the present age, and the age to come which drew near in the ministry, death and exaltation of Jesus, and which is a real part of the world in which we live today. After the third lecture someone remarked to me that an emphasis that used to be made in the church, between the already and the not yet does not seem to be particularly prominent today. I think that this was a perceptive observation. One of the ways in which we can have this sense that the kingdom of God is among us is by taking seriously what was passionately believed by Ernst Lohmeyer, and which I mentioned in an earlier lecture, that the kingdom in our world is present in the parables and the teaching of Jesus, to which we must pay especial attention.

This brings me to the next section of this evening's lecture. You have heard me say on more than one occasion that I always feel uneasy when I read the gospels and see the simplicity and freshness of Jesus proclaiming the kingdom of God, and then compare this with the church as we find it today. The Church of England has become very much part of the establishment. It is governed by a synod which is sometimes called the church's parliament, and although it is not as bad as the Westminster parliament, it has none the less absorbed some of the less wholesome aspects of the Westminster parliament, including parties (i.e., evangelical, liberal and Ango-Catholic), party discipline, and voting upon party lines. Elections of representatives to the general synod have, in recent years, become very much a party issue within the Church of England. It is true, of course, that from time to time the Archbishops and the Bishops voice their concerns about social problems. Recently, there have been statements about the extent of poverty in Britain, and the consequences of this. Unfortunately, for most people outside the church, these are simply voices articulating what some may see as good humanitarian issues, while others may disagree violently with these opinions and think that Archbishops and Bishops should keep their noses out of such matters. What the church in its established form fails to do, unfortunately, is to convey any idea that it represents a radical alternative to the world as we know it; that its founder, Jesus of Nazareth, proclaimed the closeness and actual working of a kingdom with values that radically questioned those of the world in which we live. This sense of unease that I have has become more acute in the light of recent research upon the early Christian movement, as in the work for example of the German scholar Gerd Theissen.[36] Research on the gospel of Matthew has indicated severe tensions within the community that produced this gospel, between those who were descended from the radical and itinerant disciples of Jesus who tried to continue their radical life style and methods of preaching, and the needs of the settled Matthean community of which of these radicals were rather uneasy members.[37] How do we cope with this?

One way is by having a lively sense of church history in general, and of something of the Abbey here in particular. When we look back at the history of the church we see that from time to time there have been radical movements within it that have become dissatisfied with the church as simply a part of established states, seeking to uphold rather than to challenge their polities. The monastic movements beginning in the fourth century were one such protest, as were the various reforms of the monasteries and religious orders as they, too, grew wealthy and complacent. Here, at the Abbey, we remember our connection with Saint Norbert and the establishment of the order of White Canons which served at the Abbey for over 300 years.[38] In the post reformation period in Britain, radical groups such as the Quakers and other dissenters expressed their opposition in various ways to the religion of the established church.

From my point of view as an Old Testament scholar, it is interesting to note that at the Reformation the English church establishment justified its existence by citing the example of kings in the Old Testament such as of David, Hezekiah and

---

36 Gerd Theissen, *Die Religion der ersten Christen : eine Theorie des Urchristentums*, Gütersloh :Kaiser Gütersloher Verlagshaus, 2000.

37 U. Luz, *Die Jesusgeschichte des Matthäus,* Neukirchern-Vluyn: Neukirchener Verlag, 1993.
38 H. M. Colvin, *The White Canons in England,* Oxford, 1951

Josiah, who founded and reformed the royal cult in Jerusalem. When Edward VI came to the throne following the death of Henry VIII, he was greeted by Archbishop Cranmer as a new Josiah who would be able to purify the church according to Reformation principles. The radicals who later opposed the Anglican settlement and establishment drew extensively upon the prophetic traditions of the Old Testament, traditions which were highly critical of the kinship and indeed often of the cult. As we saw in earlier lectures, opposition to the temple and prophecies that God would destroy it, were part of the agenda of the prophets.

Knowing these things is important, because they help us to see what we are doing in a wider perspective, and we are in the unusual position at the Abbey of being an independent congregation, although within the broader Anglican Communion. We use the traditional services of the Book of Common Prayer, and I have tried to show earlier in this lecture my belief that such services have a part to play in conveying something of the numinous mystery of the worship of God. But in theology and practice, being outside the normal structures of the Church of England, we have the chance to try to embody in what we do the principles of the kingdom of God as preached by Jesus, doing this, of course, in the power of the Holy Spirit, who in the teaching of Paul, is the power of the age to come but present among us. We have tried so far at the Abbey, and not without difficulty, to break away from some of the usual ideas about democratic representation and government in what we do. We are groping towards the idea that, as the body of Christ, and as members one of another, we are working not to maintain an organisation or an institution, but to seek to be an instance of the kingdom of God as proclaimed by Jesus and empowered by his Spirit.

I want to conclude by referring to a book that was recommended to me many years ago by my philosophy teacher at Manchester, Professor Dorothy Emmet, and which has been a constant source of inspiration for over fifty years. It is entitled 'The Two Moralities' and was written by the Oxford philosopher A. D. Lindsay at the invitation of Archbishop William Temple, and was the Archbishop's Lent Book for 1940.[39] In it, Lindsay describes what he calls 'the morality of my station and its duties' meaning, the moral code which regulates the behaviour of any decent law-abiding citizen, breaches of which give society the right to punish or to exclude law-breakers from the general round of daily life. He opposes to this what he calls 'the morality of grace', which he bases on the Sermon on the Mount and the teaching of Jesus and some of the teaching of Paul, especially that on love. The morality of grace does not abolish or make unnecessary the morality of my station and its duties, but shows that alongside that morality is another, deeper, profounder way of understanding reality, without which humanity cannot achieve its divinely-intended vocation.

Without explicitly discussing the kingdom of God, although he mentions it in passing occasionally, Lindsay wonderfully describes the dialectical tension that exists in a world where the establishment of the kingdom of God in the ministry of Jesus is taken seriously, and guides the lives of those who seek to follow Jesus. There is a wonderful description of the nature and task of the church from that point of view.

> It is the function of the Church...to form a community which is a fellowship, where men can live together in relations governed by a higher standard than prevails in society at large: to show by the example of her corporate life that the fact that men are all children of one Father is a more effective fact

---

[39] A. D. Lindsay, *The Two Moralities. Our Duty to God and to Society*, London: Eyre & Spottiswoode, 1940.

than all their differences of ability and wealth and station. The actual life lived in the Church ought in itself to be a living, effective, and constructive witness against the evils and failures of society.[40]

He goes on to stress the importance of what he calls 'prophecy' which, in a good Old Testament sense, he understands to involve not so much foretelling as forthtelling.

It is also the function of the Church to produce prophets, and evidence of its vitality will be the fact that it is a school of the prophets: that the men and women who show us what society might do, who correct our blindness and indifference to the evils, are inspired by the Church's fellowship. The Church ought to go a long way to encourage liberty of prophesying, to be prepared to face all the scandal to which liberty of prophesying is bound to give rise.

Lindsay goes on to say that prophesying is an individual thing, and that although the church must support individual prophets, it cannot itself be a prophetic institution, because that is not its function. I am not sure that I agree with this. However, I agree with everything that he says a few lines further on.

The challenging and revolutionary work of a real Christianity appears first as a living, actual transformation of life. It shows as new life breaking through the old growths which have served their purpose and are ready to decay. Its beginning brings the gift, not of a devastating clearance, a vacant institutionalism, but of a fresh green leaf significant of a new birth, a renewal of the spirit of life and love.

That is a splendid description of some of the effects of the kingdom of God!

---

[40] Lindsay, *Two Moralities*, p. 109.

APPENDIX

Unpublished introductory notes by Rudolf Otto for his book *The Philosophy of Religion Based on Kant and Fries* (London 1931), an English translation of *Kantische-Fries'sche Religionsphilosophie* (Tübingen 1909).

[The following four pages were written by Rudolf Otto for the 1931 English translation of *Kantische-Fries'sche Religionsphilosophie*, but were not included in that edition. They were printed on a single folded sheet of paper and inserted as an addendum into the book.

Last year, whilst investigating the influence of J. F. Fries on Leonard Nelson for the Coleridge in Wales project, Otto's *Philosophy of Religion Based on Kant and Fries* was consulted and these loose-leaf introductory notes fell out. Otto's view, expressed in these unpublished notes, that his celebrated 1909 book *The Idea of the Holy* "could scarcely offer much that was novel" to Coleridge's readers has had scant attention.

Coleridge walked around Wales in 1794 dreaming of creating an ideal society called Pantisocracy. L.S.H. Wright in his book *Samuel Taylor Coleridge and the Anglican Church* (University of Notre Dame Press, 2010) suggests Coleridge's vision was rooted in explorations of the Kingdom of God, so the inclusion here, as an appendix, of Otto's unpublished thoughts for an English language readership seems most appropriate.

A further point of note is the coincidence of Otto's remarks on Fries and de Wette with the full discussion of their work in John Rogerson's biography of de Wette, which was started, and largely undertaken, independently of Otto[41].

RMP]

---

[41] J.W. Rogerson, *W.M.L. de Wette, Founder of Modern Biblical Criticism. An Intellectual Biography*, (Journal for the Study of the Old Testament Supplement Series 126),Sheffield: JSOT Press, 1992.

The Philosophy of Religion.

AUTHOR'S NOTES ON THE TRANSLATION

THE translator, to whom my best thanks are due, kindly permits the following observations on his work:

1. The book was written in 1909 (new edition published in 1921). Not long before, in an exposition and criticism of W. Wundt's *Theory of Religion*, I had begun to give expression to my ideas on the non-rational factor in Religion; these were afterwards developed in my book, *The Idea of the Holy*. In *The Philosophy of Religion* I wished to present the "rational" factor in Religion, which, for me, is no less important and essential than the non-rational.

2. For this purpose I expounded the philosophy of religion as taught by J. F. Fries, supplemented by the thought of De Wette, who, next to Schleiermacher, was the founder in Germany of that "Modern Theology" which, in its fundamental ideas, I myself follow. My later writings will show how their teachings have developed in my own thought.

3. The traditional theology had long ago drawn a distinction between *revelatio generalis* and *revelatio specialis*. In these two terms there is a problem as profound as it is difficult: on the one hand we have the conviction that religion, and our own particular religion, lays claim to universal validity and therefore appeals to general and necessary principles of theoretical and practical reason; and on the other hand religion is based on the pure contingence of great historical data, which as "facts of revelation" possess a value, and cannot be constructed by any *a priori* reasoning. Christian Theology is only possible if both these factors are recognised in their connection and reciprocal action; for without the *a priori* factor it lapses into more [mere ?] emotionalism, and without the contingent-historical element it loses its central and characteristic import as a religion of redemption and

87

salvation. Theologians will dispute this problem, the *a priori* and General versus the Contingent and Historical till the end of things; and it is perhaps a matter of doubt whether a satisfactory final solution of the problem will ever be found. In my opinion, however, a combination of the principles of Fries with those of De Wette and Schleiermacher seems to offer a solution, which, although it does not appear to me as a final oracular statement, has given me a provisional Archimedian δός μοι,, ποῦ στῶ, a ground that I can still rest upon.

4. Two considerations have induced me to lay this attempt before the British public, if indeed in all reserve. Firstly, the favourable reception accorded to other of my works, and the desire that I may not be misunderstood through these works. On *no account* do I wish to be considered a "non-rationalist". In all religion, and in my own religion, I indeed recognise the profundity of the non-rational factor; but this deepens my conviction that it is the duty of serious theology to win as much ground as it can for *Ratio* in this realm, and even at the point where our rational concepts desert us, to satisfy the demands of judicious theological teaching by framing "ideograms" as accurately as possible, where dogmatic concepts are impossible. And secondly, I hope that there will be understanding for Fries and De Wette in the country of *Samuel Taylor Coleridge.* For me it is a fortunate omen that my book appears at almost the same time as the excellent monograph of J.H. Muirhead, *Coleridge as a Philosopher.* The remarkable analogies in Coleridge and Fries became patent to me, soon after the appearance of my own book, through a study of C. Broicher on *Anglican Theology from Coleridge to Robertson.* It appears to me that Coleridge in his poems had already reached such a clear vision of the factor of the "Numinous" and had so clearly expressed this vision, that to readers of this poet my book on *The Idea of the Holy* could scarcely offer much that was novel. This point has been well put by John Harvey in Appendix 10 of *The Idea of the Holy.*

5. One of my critics predicted that in time to come a more accurate "psychological" investigation would prove that the Idea of God is a fundamental element in our thought. If this is taken, not as referring to the specific content of the Christian idea of God, but to the fundamental theistic conception of a real and primal unity transcending the universe, then the Friesan philosophy may claim that it fulfils this prediction.

6. As to the relation of Fries and Schleiermacher, I would refer my readers to my criticism of these thinkers in *Mysticism East and West* (now being published by Macmillan, New York) and in my *Religious Essays* (now being published by Oxford University Press).

7. As to the translation itself, I would suggest the following addenda:

Page 17. – I found the announcement of a treatise on the significance of gloves in the history of religion.

Page 23. – The German expression "Gefühl" is not quite "emotion". "Gefühl" can mean a form of cognizance in an unconceptional or preconceptional way. In this sense "Gefühl" is acknowledged by Fries as a possible source of cognizances apart from sensual or conceptual cognizances.

Page 24. – "Proof" and "proving". We have in German the possibility of distinguishing between "beweisen" and "begründen." Fries expects a "Begründung" for any form of conviction, but he rejects the rationalistic preconception, that proof in the form of logical "beweisen" is the only valid form of "Begründung" for our convictions. See also "proof" in chapter vii.

Page 24 (footnote). – Here the distinction of "Erkennen" and "Wissen" is important. "Erkennen" is *cognoscere*, "Wissen" is *scire*. *Deus non scitur* – as the Sorbonne already had decreed, and quite rightly; but certainly *Deus cognoscitur*, viz. *fide*. The English terms "knowledge" and "knowing" seem to me to refer merely to *scire* as *scienta*. Theology is not a *scienta* of God, but certainly must claim to offer a *cognito* of God. See also page 43. – A world of faith can be opposed to a world of *scienta*, but ought not to be opposed to a world of *cognito*. Without this distinction it would be misleading to use the word "knowledge" on page 68, Foundation of Ideal Knowledge. Ideal Knowledge is no *scienta*, but it is *cognition*. See also page 99. – Faith stands in opposition to "knowledge" as *scienta*, but faith, when a "begründete Überzeungung" claims to be a *cognito*.

Page 135. – "Ahnung" is not so much "man's deepest longing and need" as a "Gefühl," in the sense mentioned above. It comes very near to what I have described in *The Idea of the Holy* as "divination."

Page 151. – Schleiermacher and De Wette were certainly not leaders of a "theology of compromise." "Vermittlungs-theologie," which was a name for a very important school of modern theological thought, I would rather venture to render by "theology of mediation." Schleiermacher and De Wette did for their time what Clement of Alexandria and Origen did for the ancient Easter Church; what the Anglican Humanistic fathers did for their age; they established a "mediation" between the spiritual culture of their time and Christian thought. Superseding the shallowness of rationalism, they attempted and succeeded in keeping the best results of the great period of "Aufklärung" and in combining them, without lapsing into traditionalism and primitive orthodoxy, with the spiritual inheritance of historical Christianity. Therefore they were called "mediators." The translator uses afterwards the word "theology of *reconciliation*." This word appears to be more to the point than "compromise." De Wette was "uncompromising as possible.

To the translator and publisher alike I render my due thanks.

RUDOLF OTTO.

MARBURG A. L.

BIBLIOGRAPHY

Barrett, C. K. *The Holy Spirit and the Gospel Tradition*, London: SPCK, 1966.

Barrett, C. K. *The Gospel According to St. John. An Introduction with Commentary and Notes on the Greek Text*, London: SPCK, 1958

Barrett, C. K. *The First Epistle to the Corinthians* (Black's New Testament Commentaries), London: A. & C. Black, 1968

Bayle, P. *A General Dictionary, Historical and Critical*, (trans. J. P. Bernard, et al.), London, 1736

Clutton-Brock, A. *What is the Kingdom of Heaven?*, London: Methuen, 1919.

Colvin, H. M. *The White Canons in England*, Oxford: Clarendon Press, 1951

DeVries, S. J. *Yesterday, Today and Tomorrow. Time and History in the Old Testament*, London: SPCK, 1975

Dietrich, W., C. Link, *Die dunklen Seiten Gottes. Band 2, Allmacht und Ohnmacht*, Neukirchen-Vluyn: Neukirchener Verlag, 2000

Ebeling, G. *The Nature of Faith*, London: Collins, 1966

Frankfort, H. *Kingship and the Gods. A Study of Ancient Near Eastern Religion as the Integration of Society & Nature*, Chicago: University of Chicago Press, 1948

Green, R. L., W. Hooper, *C. S. Lewis. A Biography*, London: Collins, 1974

Haenchen, E. 'Johanneische Probleme' in *Zeitschrift für Theologie und Kirche*, 56 (1959), pp. 19-54

Hartenstein, F., B. Janowski, *Psalmen* (Biblischer Kommentar Altes Testament XV/1), Neukirchen-Vluyn: Neukirchener Verlag, 2012

Jüngel, E. *Paulus und Jesus. Eine Untersuchung zur Präzisierung der Frage nach dem Urpsrung der Christologie,* Tübingen: Mohr Siebeck, 7th ed., 20

Kirkpatrick, A. F. *The Book of Psalms,* Cambridge: Cambridge University Press, vol. 1, 1930

Lewis, C. S. *The Pilgrim's Regress, An Allegorical Apology for Christianity, Reason and Romanticism,* London: HarperCollins, 1998

Lindsay, A. D. *The Two Moralities. Our Duty to God and to Society,* London: Eyre & Spottiswoode, 1940

Lohmeyer, E. *Kultus und Evangelium,* Göttingen: Kommissionsverlag Vandenhoeck & Ruprecht, 1942

Lohmeyer, E. 'Vom Sinn der Gleichnisse Jesu' in E. Lohmeyer, *Urchristliche Mystik. Neutestamentliche Studien,* Darmstadt: Wissenschaftliche Buchgesellschaft, 1958, pp.123-157

Luther, M. Großer Katechismus, in *Die Bekenntnisschriften der evangelisch-lutherischen Kirche,* Göttingen: Vandenhoeck & Ruprecht, 1979

Luz, U. *Das Evangelium nach Matthäus (Evangelisch-Katholischer Kommentar zum Neuen Testament),* Zürich: Benzinger Verlag; Neukirchen-Vluyn: Neukirchener Verlag, I/3, 1997,

Luz, U. *Die Jesusgeschichte des Matthäus,* Neukirchern-Vluyn: Neukirchener Verlag, 1993

Marsden, G. M. *Fundamentalism and American Culture. The Shaping of Twentieth Century Evangelicalism 1870-1925,* New York: Oxford University Press 1980

Morgenthaler, R. *Statistik des neutestamentlichen Wortschatzes,* Zürich: Gotthelf-Verlag, 1958

Otto, R. *Das Heilige.Über das Irrationale in der Idee des Göttlichen und sein Verhältnis zum Rationalen,* Munich: C. H. Beck, 1917, ET *The Idea of the Holy. An Inquiry into the Non-rational Factor in the Idea of the Divine and its relations to the Rational,* Harmondsworth: Penguin, 1959

Otto, R. *Kantische-Fries'sche Religionsphilosophie,* Tübingen, 1909, ET *The Philosophy of Religion,* London: Williams & Norgate, 1931

Quick, O. C. *The Realism of Christ's Parables.* Ida Hartley Lectures delivered at Colne, Lancs, October 1930, London: SCM Press, 1931

Rogerson, J.W. *W.M.L. de Wette, Founder of Modern Biblical Criticism. An Intellectual Biography,* (Journal for the Study of the Old Testament Supplement Series 126),Sheffield: JSOT Press, 1992.

Rogerson, J. W. *The Psalms in Daily Life,* London: SPCK, 2001

Rogerson, J.W. *The Holy Spirit in Biblical and Pastoral Perspective,* Sheffield: Beauchief Abbey Press, 2013

Ruskin, J. 'Of Many Things', in *Modern Painters,* vol. 3, London: George Allen, 1906

Saur, M. *Die Königspsalmen. Studien zur Entstehung und Theologie,* (Beihefte zur Zeitschrift für die alttestamentliche Wissenschaft 340), Berlin: W. De Gruyter, 2004

Schüssler, W., E. Sturm, *Paul Tillich. Leben- Werk –Wirkung,* Darmstadt: Wissenschaftliche Buchgesellschaft, 2007

Taylor, C. *Sources of the Self. The Making of the Modern Identity,* Cambridge: Cambridge University Press, 1989,

Temple, W. *Readings in St. John' Gospel,* London: Macmillan, 1952

Theissen, G. *Die Religion der ersten Christen : eine Theorie des Urchristentums,* Gütersloh :Kaiser Gütersloher Verlagshaus, 2000

Thomas, J. H. *Paul Tillich. An Appraisal,* London: SCM Press, 1963

INDEX

About the Author
J. W. Rogerson

John William Rogerson was born in London in 1935 and educated at Bec School, Tooting, the Joint Services School for Linguists, Coulsdon Common, where he completed an intensive course in Russian, and the Universities of Manchester, Oxford and Jerusalem, where he studied theology and Semitic languages. He was ordained in 1964 and served as Assistant Curate at St. Oswald's, Durham. From 1964 to 1975 he was Lecturer, and from 1975 to 1979 Senior Lecturer in Theology at Durham University before moving in 1979 to become Professor and Head of the Department of Biblical Studies at the University of Sheffield, retiring in 1996. He was made an honorary Canon of Sheffield Cathedral in 1982 and an Emeritus Canon in 1995. In addition to many essays and scholarly articles, his published books include *Myth in Old Testament Interpretation* (1974), *Psalms* (Cambridge Bible Commentary, with J.W. McKay, 1977), *Anthropology and the Old Testament* (1978), *Old Testament Criticism in the Nineteenth Century: England and Germany* (1984), *The New Atlas of the Bible* (1985, translated into nine languages), *W. M. L . de Wette., Founder of Modern Biblical Criticism. An Intellectual Biography* (1991), *The Bible and Criticism in Victorian Britain. Profiles of F. D. Maurice and William Robertson Smith* (1995), *An Introduction to the Bible* (1999, 3rd edition 2012), *Theory and Practice in Old Testament Ethics* (2004), *According to the Scriptures? The Challenge of using the Bible in Social, Moral and Political Questions* (2007), *A Theology of the Old Testament. Cultural memory, communication and being human* (2009), *The Art of Biblical Prayer* (2011). He was awarded the degree of Doctor of Divinity for published work by the University of Manchester in 1975, and has also been awarded the Honorary Degree of Doctor of Divinity by the University of Aberdeen and the Honorary Degree of Dr. theol. by the Friedrich-Schiller-Universität, Jena and the Albert-Ludwigs-Universität, Freiburg im Breisgau.

Other books by Beauchief Abbey Press

ON BEING A BROAD CHURCH by John Rogerson

On Being a Broad Church explores the social vision and work of the influential 19th century Broad Church movement led by the writer of The Water Babies Charles Kingsley and active campaigner and visionary churchman F.D. Maurice. This engaging series of lectures are presented here in a survey that reveals the importance of the broad church movement for contemporary Christian faith.

THE HOLY SPIRIT
IN BIBLICAL AND PASTORAL PERSPECTIVE
by John Rogerson

The Holy Spirit in Biblical and Pastoral Perspective is a scholarly review of all biblical references to the Holy Spirit, and an exploration of the implications and benefits to congregations of approaches to teaching, learning and interpretation when the Holy Spirit is understood, not as a Power, but as a relationship with a Person. The book carefully examines the Bible, including the Old Testament, for texts including reference to the Holy Spirit and offers readers who may be familiar with thinking that presents the Holy Spirit as only being manifest in signs or wonders, or working through elders and leaders, the assurance that, where the Gospel is faithfully preached and received, God is at work on the inside of his creation in the Holy Spirit.

UNEXPECTED DISCOVERY by John Rogerson

Unexpected Discovery is a collection of sermons given by John Rogerson that tackle head-on major issues of church and faith in the 21st century, dealing with the miracles and mission of Jesus, social justice, angels, God's dealings with fraudsters and the essential public role of Christian religion in a collection that teaches, questions and proclaims traditional Christianity at the heart of modern living.

www.beauchiefabbeypress.org.uk